In Praise of Devon

The old Devon: Middlecott above Chagford, 1982.

In Praise
of Devon

A Guide to its People, Places and Character

John Lane

Green Books

CONTENTS

Introduction   8

1. THE FACE OF THE COUNTRY

The Devon Landscape   14
The Rivers of Devon   16
The Coastline of Devon   18
Lynton   20
Clovelly   22
Dartmoor   24
Exmoor   26

2. ANIMAL, VEGETABLE, MINERAL

Devonshire Rain   30
Dartmoor Ponies   32
Great Trees   34
The Devon Lane   36
Some Devonshire Gardens   38
The Lustleigh Orchard   40
Lee Moor Clay Works   42

3. PLACE

Towns & Villages

Exeter   46
Bideford   48
Torquay   50
Totnes   52
Plymouth   54
Appledore   56
Cornworthy's Natural History   58

Buildings

Holy Wells   60
Stone Circles on Dartmoor   62
A Mediæval Pulpit   64
St. Mary's, Atherington   66
St. Mary's, Honeychurch   68
Exeter Cathedral   70
Dartington Hall   72
The Dartmoor Longhouse   74
Cadhay   76
Loughwood Meeting House   78
The Adam Rooms at Saltram   80
All Saints, Babbacombe   82
Castle Drogo   84
The Dream Church of Milber   86

4. IMAGES & OBJECTS

A Prehistoric Wooden Figure   90
A Roman Bronze Figure   92
Mediæval Ironwork   94
Beatus and Bosses   96

Harvest Jugs	98
Devon Clocks	100
Honiton Lace	102
Blake at Arlington	104
The Staverton Parish Map	106

5. TRADITIONS

Church Bells in Devon	110
Decorating the Parish Church	112
Devon Cider	114
The Village Pub	116
Devonshire Dialect	118
Cob and Thatch	120
The Circling Year	122
Clotted Cream	124
Song and Dance	126

6. OCCUPATIONS

Farming	130
Mining and Extraction	132
The Cloth Industry	134
Fishing	136
The Building Industry	138
The Great Western Railway	140
New Business	142

7. DEVONSHIRE CHARACTERS

Robert Herrick, poet	146
Arscott of Tetcott, squire	148
Sabine Baring-Gould, squire, parson, writer	149
Henry Williamson, writer	151
Ivor Bourne, retired farmer	152
Clive Bowen, potter	154
Sheila Cassidy, doctor, healer, writer	155
Roderick & Gillie James, architect and quilter	158
Reg & Hazel Kingsland, farmworker and wife	160
James & Sandy Lovelock, scientist and wife	162
James Marshall, thatcher	165
John Moat, poet, novelist	166
Ernest Mold, retired doctor	168
Joyce Molyneux, cook	170
Charles Napier, rector	171
Ady & Vanessa Nuthall, farmer and cook	174
Peter Randall-Page, sculptor	176
Anna Robertson, voluntary worker	178
Peter Smith, shopkeeper	180
Paul Wharton, fisherman	182
Further Reading	184
Index	187

First published in 1998 by Green Books Ltd,
Foxhole, Dartington, Totnes, Devon TQ9 6EB

Copyright © John Lane 1998

The right of John Lane to be identified as author of this work has been asserted
in accordance with sections 77 and 78 of the Copyright Designs and Patents Act 1988

Book and cover design by Rick Lawrence

Typeset in Berling and Bembo Italic at Green Books

Origination & printing by Kingfisher Print & Design, Totnes, Devon

Bound by Folio Bookbinders, Bristol

A catalogue record for this book is available from the British Library

ISBN 1 870098 75 7

The Publishers would like to thank the Environment Agency for making a grant towards the
production costs of this book, and the following for permission to reproduce photographs, or
photographs of materials in their possession: Chris Chapman, frontispiece; Courtauld Gallery, pages
20 and 57; Liz Tainton and the Beaford Photographic Archive, pages 31, 111, 118, 124, 127, 132, 136 &
139; Bernard Samuels, page 36; Exeter City Museums, pages 46, 91, 93, 98 & 100; Burton Art Gallery
and Museum, Bideford, page 48; Torre Abbey, page 51; Reg Barker, page 58; Mrs Edward Piper, pages
62 and 63; Peter Burton, page 67; National Trust Photographic Library and Andreas von Einsiedel,
pages 81 and 104; National Trust Photographic Library and Derrick E. Witty, page 84; National Trust
Photographic Library and Niall Clutton, page 85; Harland Walshaw, page 94; the Dean and Chapter
of Exeter Cathedral, pages 96 and 97; City and County of Swansea, Swansea Museum Collection,
page 99; James Ravilious and the Beaford Photographic Archive, pages 122 & 131; Dartington Rural
Archive, page 130; Morwellham and Tamar Valley Trust, page 133; Science and Society Picture
Library, page 141; Royal Cornwall Museum, page 148; Henry Williamson Literary Estate, page 151;
Keith Duncan, page 154; Kim Sayer, pages 158 and 159.

Acknowledgements

In writing this book, I have relied in different ways on the assistance of a great number of people. The debt I owe to the researches of others—and in particular the studies of W.G. Hoskins—is almost beyond calculation. Other books which have been helpful are referred to in the Further Reading section. I thank Arnold Bradbury, Claire Ash Wheeler, Peter Burton, Chris Cleaves, Andrea Foxwell, Michael Gee, Laurence Golding, Ralph Hare, Sir Peter Laurence, Moira Mellor, June Mitchell, Bridget and Mischa Norland, Father John Potter, Jose Reddaway, Robin Ravilious, Bernard Samuels, John Stevens-Guille, Vicky Schilling, Harland Walshaw, John West, Ian Woodford and Betty Wilkins for all kinds of assistance, large and small. I also thank James Ravilious for his help in selecting my photographs, John Elford and Satish Kumar for their constructively sympathetic editing, and my wife, Truda, for her continuous support. I would also like to thank those whose names are mentioned in the following pages. Some were friends, others complete strangers who welcomed me into their homes and co-operated with interest, patience and kindness.

To enhance a book in praise of Devon, I have chosen to use the work of two of its most distinguished photographers: Chris Chapman (frontispiece) and James Ravilious (pages 122 and 131), both of whom have made loving and extensive records of different parts of the county. Otherwise, with only a few exceptions, the photographs are my own. To avoid the visual degradation of our culture is no easy matter; scarcely anywhere can one look without seeing something intrusive and ugly. Wherever possible I have tried to avoid landscapes and streets, buildings and views that are defaced with telephone poles, assorted notices, vehicles and street signs. The result is, I admit, somewhat idealised.

INTRODUCTION

Every continent has its own great spirit of place. Every people is polarised in some particular locality, which is home, the homeland. Different places on the face of the earth have different vital effluence, different vibration, different chemical exhilaration, different polarity with different stars: call it what you like. But the spirit of place is a great reality.

D.H. Lawrence, Studies in Classic American Literature.

Devon invites and defies definition. No sooner has one crossed its boundaries, than one experiences a difference. Unmistakably it is a singular territory. And yet this singularity, so easy to detect, is hard to pin down and classify. The visitor may think he or she has captured it, made it last for ever, but it soon withers away, eludes one's grasp, or is contradicted by a different impression.

For Devon, although a domain of its own, is a thousand different things. It is her deep-cut lanes, her wild hedgerow flowers, her cob and thatch cottages, her special products and peculiarities of speech. It is her secret, hidden valleys and combes, her rain-washed skies, her husbanded landscapes. It is her deep-rooted conservatism, her independence and isolation. All this and much besides, may help to characterise the 'real' Devon—something quintessential, undiluted, unmistakable, but at the same time intangible and elusive. Consider the ravishing South Hams, luxuriant and

bosky; the heart-easing beauty of the Teign valley or the gentle entrance to the River Dart. Look, too, at the leafy corbels in the nave of the most forest-like of all the English cathedrals, Exeter; the densely carved foliage on the screens of a dozen Devon churches, or the serenity of Chagford and Colyton. Each is different from the other, yet at the same time shares an indefinable essence—something verdant and melodious, stable, rooted deep in the soil. This essence is the 'real' Devon. No wonder that those of us who live in the county take for granted that it is one of the chief wonders of the world.

Doubtless there are landscapes which contradict this luxuriance. There is the granite boss of Dartmoor. There is the iron coast south of Hartland. There is the scraggy country between Bradworthy and Holsworthy, austere and impoverished. Yet these are are in the minority. Devon's overall beauty, unassailable tranquillity, slow pace of time and ancient pattern of agricultural settlement, summon up an archetype which is as unforgettable as it is rare. We say 'Devon' and picture an almost utopian vision of strong and often wooded hills, verdant valleys and umbrageous trees. Maybe it is raining and the landscape is a panoramic sweep; maybe there are pylons and a few bungalows... never mind, we have only to travel a little further to find the real 'Devon'. For if it did not already exist we would have had to invent it.

One can approach the county as an historian, an ecclesiologist, a botanist, an architect or as an antiquarian. My own approach has been visual, unashamedly personal and celebratory. *In Praise of Devon* makes not the remotest attempt to be comprehensive—there is simply too much to do justice to it all—or representative. I am in fact only too conscious of what is missing. There is nothing about the sizeable increase of the population in recent years. Nothing about sport or music, geology and education. Nothing either about Devon's growing dependence on tourism and its contemporary problems: its lack of a balanced population, low-cost rural housing, adequate public transport and employment opportunities for the young. Falling agricultural prices are also creating a crisis for the county's many farmers. The consequences for Devon could be tragic—it may drive many from the land, unsettle whole communities and further impoverish both the landscape and an authentic local culture.

Therefore those looking for an overall picture of the county's contemporary life might be advised to look elsewhere. For as its title suggests, *In Praise of Devon* is a guide to a selection of the county's people, places and character, and very little else. It includes quite a lot of history, a smattering of topography and, I hope, a feeling for the character of the whole. However, it is (inevitably) selective. To have attempted to broaden its range would have resulted in a different kind of book from the one I set out to present—one intentionally and unashamedly positive.

Affirmation of this kind can be neither universal nor indiscriminate. I have sometimes therefore felt the need to criticise that which I thought to be standardising, drab and insensitive. A great deal of beauty and distinction yet remains throughout Devon, but impersonality and ugliness are afoot. So often I found a twentieth-century 'development'—a multi-storey car park or a sprawl of new suburban houses—impossible to praise. Undeniably, these things may serve important social purposes, but do they need to do so in such an insensitive way? Do they have to be so drably uniform, so vulgarly out of keeping with their environment, so unconscious of their effect on the 'real' Devon? The French writer Simone Weil commented that: "The essential characteristic of the twentieth century is the growing weakness, and almost the disappearance, of the idea of value. This is one of those rare phenomena, as far as one can tell, to be really new in human society." Having travelled all over the county, I can only agree with her.

Weil's contemporary, the poet David Jones, once distinguished between the pre-industrial world and the centuries which followed it. He called it The Break. Without any conscious decision to do so, I think *In Praise of Devon* may reveal a prejudice in favour of pre-industrial rural England. I have, of course, no wish to idealise those times: much of it was, I know, imperfect and unjust, sometimes violent and for many, back-breaking in its uneaseful toil. I also realise how dangerous it is to hanker after what has passed. Life is continuously changing. Nonetheless, I love and continue to admire the centuries when we employed our aesthetic faculty to such good effect; when, too, there was an organic relationship with the land, when life moved at a leisurely speed and there was a shared sense of place. Of the mediæval period, so often sensual and earthy, yet soaring and cosmic, there remain a great many buildings—churches and almshouses amongst them. And of the later centuries, so often harmonious and proportionate and with a comeliness absent from our more thrusting times, there also remains much unspoiled, modest architecture, and amply enough to sustain an atmosphere.

There is also much that is admirable about the modern industrialised world, but that is surely no reason to be complacent about its weaknesses and failures as far as the county is concerned. These include its impoverishing and standardising effects which have already done so much to despoil and erode the Devon countryside, the Devon settlement and the Devon culture. Some aspects of these—like the brash new service stations and the out-of-town supermarkets—are imposed by national and multi-national companies more bent on profit than the preservation of local character. Others are introduced by county-based builders, architects, shopkeepers, administrators and, not least, by the Local Authorities. An example of the latter is the nine-storey tower of offices forced onto Barnstaple in 1968 by decision-makers in the County Council, an atrocious act of insensitivity very hard to understand or forgive. Nonetheless, it is not only the big players; we all play our part, adding to or subtracting from our inheritance. We may choose to ignore what is happening or resist it. We may choose to buy something, alter something, build something or plant something which in its own way is no less considerate towards the character of 'Devon' than Barnstaple's alien imposition. No: next time let us reflect upon the consequences of our action before we act. Let us address the effect of our decision on the distinctive character of a locality. Let us leave behind features with which our successors will be delighted. To do so is not nostalgia but common sense.

THE BOOK IS DIVIDED into seven thematic sections. The first introduces the physical nature of the county—the durable realities which have shaped the county's life for millions of years. The second touches on a variety of natural phenomena: trees, ponies, gardens, rain and clay. Chapter Three is about Place: the towns and villages where people live, and the buildings they have made and are using today. The next chapter, Images & Objects, introduces a small selection of Devon artifacts and the pleasures we can gain from them. Chapters Five and Six feature a selection of the traditions and occupations intrinsic to and descriptive of Devon's peculiar genius. The final chapter is composed of sketches of contemporary people who are adding to the texture, the weave and quality of this richly subtle land.

The reader may approach the reading of this book in any way he or she chooses—either by starting at the beginning and working through to the end or by dipping into it as the fancy strikes, or a mixture of both. Either way the result should be the same. In writing *In Praise of Devon*, I have tried to do justice to the range, vitality and variety of its subject. I hope you will find it as enjoyable to read as it was to prepare.

Stepping stones at Week Ford, near Hexworthy Bridge.

CHAPTER ONE:

The Face of the Country

Even beneath the stormy skies of a wet, unseasonable April, perhaps no English county that I have seen is quite so lovely as this land of Devon.

H. Rider Haggard, c.1900

Sheep and oak tree, above the Torridge valley near Beaford.

THE DEVON LANDSCAPE

Devon, even up to the coming of the railways, was a county of isolated communities, secret and remote. Geology and topography have played their part; history and distance from London have also contributed towards the creation of what has been described as the most amenable county in Britain. For even though ravishing panoramas and areas of spectacular wildness are common enough, the popular idea of Devon as a county of steeply banked lanes, hidden villages and embosomed farms, is not far from the truth. The countryside's main characteristic is its comfort, its sense of intimacy, its security. Devonshire is an unforbidding, amply domesticated place in which to live. It is a landscape where one can always feel at home.

Nevertheless, it is not a single entity. The poet and song writer Theo Marzials described the country around Colyton as a "landscape of endless and immediate variety". And this is as true of this district, which I once so often walked, as of Devon as a whole. There is the rich farmland of the New Red Sandstone with its steep hedgerows stuffed with luxuriant growths, but also the windier and scraggier landscape of the culm country around Holsworthy in the north-west. There are the snug villages of warm thatch, green and gold with lichen and moss, but also villages of cold stone with thin, gaunt church towers. There are the dumpy hills towards Tiverton, the wooded valleys and clear rivers of the South Hams but also a coastline of gaunt cliffs where Atlantic breakers burst upon black rocks. Then, above all else, there is Dartmoor,

Ashwell, near Dolton, in late spring.

defining and at the same time contradicting everything we think the county is or should be about. It is the master-key to the topography of Devon, a broken tableland of sweeping shallows, fleshy granite outcrops and wooded river valleys; moody, spectacular yet strangely introverted. In the north, too, the county is obstructed by Exmoor, another bare plateau of almost equal altitude made up not of granite but layers of hard sedimentary rocks, sandstones, slates and limestones.

Although the geological measures of Devon range from volcanic granite to red sandstone and soft cretaceous strata in East Devon, all share the common attribute of lending themselves to the formation of mud. The existence of masses of high land, the fact that the peninsula is well thrust into the mild, rain-bearing winds of the Atlantic, and the number of river estuaries running far inland, have all helped to encourage the formation of a mild, wet climate with rapidly changing weather. In the centuries before railroads and turnpikes, a journey of a few miles was something of a major expedition. Little wonder that Jane Austen wrote in terms of entry "into Devonshire" as if the journey into the county were like a forage into an unknown land.

Such factors have increased the distinctive character of the county's towns and parishes, each of which has developed its own independence of character. To this day, Barnstaple and Bideford are rivals—and someone living in Dartmouth has probably never visited either. Thus it is that North Devon, with few towns and a bracing climate, is strikingly different from the south, which has many towns and generally more clement weather; while West Devon is also markedly different from the eastern side of the county.

Beyond Dowland, looking towards Iddesleigh. Dartmoor in the distance.

THE RIVERS OF DEVON

*The confluence of the East Webburn and West Webburn
rivers between Ponsworthy and Buckland-in-the-Moor.*

Taw and Torridge, Teign and Exe, Dart and Tamar, Otter and Axe, Avon and Erme—rising in remote moors and hills, flowing over the land, moving through forests and small villages, Devon's many rivers have had an enormous significance, not only for the landscape but also because of the part they have played in people's lives. They have harboured legend, fostered myth, provided nourishment and energy. Their characters and histories are equally varied. There are those that are maternal and languorous in their flow; those that seem cold and aloof or are gentle and seductive; rivers that boil over with a furious, destructive power: rivers that are grave and rivers that are impulsive. Each carries its own range of moods.

Many of the Devon rivers have names of the greatest antiquity, and since they are very old, their meaning is not always known. The Bovey, Clyst, Erme, or Tamar and several others belong to this category. On the other hand it is known that the Axe and Exe got their names from the Celtic word meaning 'fish'—almost certainly salmon, since in prehistoric times the Devonshire rivers probably swarmed with salmon like the Canadian rivers of today. The river Dart originates from the British word meaning 'oak', in all probability because its steep-sided valley was lined with dense oak-woods. Like so many other Devon rivers, it rises on Dartmoor, to which it gives its name.

The river Okement (on which Okehampton stands) receives its name from two British words, meaning 'swift and noisy'; on the other hand the river Taw, one of the two great North Devon rivers, means 'the silent one'. Its sister, the Torridge, means ' the violent, rough stream', and so it can be today, especially after winter rains. According to W.G. Hoskins, other rivers were given evocative names whose significance is no longer clear: the Yealm, which means 'kind', the Carey, which means 'friendly,' the Kenn, which means 'brilliant' or 'shining', and the Dalch, which contributes to the Taw, which means 'black or dark stream'. These names would have been known to our ancestors before the Roman invasion.

The narrow valleys of Dartmoor carry the shallow streams which are the headwaters of the majority of Devon's great rivers. Some, such as the Dart and Teign, flow south-east, whilst the Taw and the Torridge wind generally northwards out to sea; in fact the Torridge rises on the same ridge as the Tamar. It is over fifty miles in length, with four main tributaries: the Waldon, Lew, Okement and Mere. The Tamar, for much of its length the boundary between Devon and Cornwall, begins its life almost on the North coast, finally joining the sea at Plymouth.

Near Ashprington, looking towards Totnes. The winding river is the Dart.

THE COASTLINE OF DEVON

Devon is one of only three English counties—Cornwall and Kent being the other two—to possess a north and a south coast, and, with the exception of Cornwall, it has the greatest proportion of coastline to area of any English county. The sea has therefore played an exceptionally large part in its climate and history from the Bronze age onwards.

Devon is connected to the rest of England by a narrow neck of land between the mouth of the Parrett on the north coast and Lyme Regis on the south, a distance of only thirty five miles. Beyond this neck, the peninsula of south-western England thrusts westwards into the Atlantic for about 130 miles, widening into a solid block in Devon, more than seventy miles across, and then tapering rapidly down the length of Cornwall.

But it is not only the extent but the variety of Devon's coastline which is spectacular; and the best—indeed the only—way to enjoy it, is by walking.

Starting at Foreland Point, east of Lynton, the northern coast rises to Butter Hill, almost a thousand feet above the silver of Lynmouth Bay, then travels westwards towards Woody Bay with its panorama of South Wales across the Bristol Channel. Moving towards Ilfracombe the cliffs are hump-backed, rounded with steep slopes covered with grass and other vegetation reaching down almost to the sea. This is a section which contains some of the most spectacular coastal scenery in Britain, indeed in Europe.

Moving southwards towards the estuary of the Taw, there is beauty of a different kind: the great ochre crescent of Woolacombe sands and, at Braunton Burrows, wastes of unstable hillocky dunes and grass as deserted and eerie as a landscape on the moon. The great wide-open estuaries of the rivers Taw and Torridge are beautiful, as is the pebble ridge and two-mile length of sand at Westward Ho!; the stretch of coast from Buck's Mills to the bold headland of

Near Marsland Cliff, Welcombe, looking north towards Hartland Point.

Hartland Point (mentioned by the second century geographer Ptolemy as the Hercules Promontory) is no less spectacular. Here, the distant hump of Lundy can be seen rising out of the sea.

Turning south towards Cornwall, walking up and down the steep grassy hillsides—up and then down, up and down—the prospect of the jagged saw-edged black rocks jutting out into the sea below and the endless rollers, with their high feathery crests advancing towards land, are of great beauty. It is a cliffscape of stupendous power but alleviated, at least in early summer, by the delicate abundance of wild flowers: pink thrift, cadmium-bright yellow gorse, bird's-foot trefoil, foxgloves, and in damp spots, the tall yellow iris.

The southern coast is very different: less wild, less barren and far more populated, with not only Plymouth on the great creek of The Sound but the seaside resorts of Brixham, Paignton, Torquay, Dawlish, Teignmouth, Budleigh Salterton, Sidmouth, Beer and Seaton, parading their charms for the benefit of migrant summer visitors. There is much to admire along the 150 miles of this coast: Salcombe Estuary, sheltered, south-facing, luxuriant and balmy; the striking headland of the Start, whose massive cliffs have quartz veins running through the dark rock; the two-mile crescent of Slapton sands and the remarkable freshwater lake, Slapton Ley. The cliffs at Bolt Head, Outer Froward Point and from Beer Head towards Sidmouth, are also exceptionally fine.

Near Berry Head, Torbay, looking westwards towards Sharkham Point.

LYNTON

'From the Castle Hotel, Lynton' by Samuel Palmer., 1834.
The original belongs to the Courtauld Institute Galleries, London.

The scenery of this parish is of exceptional charm; it includes the East Lyn river, Lyn Cleave and the so-called Valley of the Rocks. Yet these places, like the 600-foot-high cliff whose brow Lynton crowns—were all but unknown to anyone but their own inhabitants for countless hundreds of years. Then, quite suddenly, they were 'discovered'. This was during the Napoleonic wars, when access to the Continent was closed and a trickle of English visitors in search of wild, romantic scenery came here for the first time.

Travel for these visitors was far from easy (coaches took almost a day to cover the thirty-nine miles from Exeter to Barnstaple), but undeterred they came, and have continued to do so in increasing numbers ever since. To accommodate them, the first hotel in Lynton was built in 1807, but most travellers stayed in 'cottages', of which many attractive examples still remain.

Two of the earliest were the banker Mr. Coutts and the Marchioness of Bute. Robert Southey also visited. He described it as "the finest spot, except Cintra and the Arrabida, that I ever saw". Apart from the poet Coleridge, who took his friend William Wordsworth to Lynmouth in 1797, another literary visitor was the nineteen-year-old Shelley, who stayed with his newly wed wife, Harriet, for nine weeks in the summer of 1812. To William Godwin he described the scenery: "This place is beautiful. . . Mountains certainly of not less perpendicular elevation than 1000 feet are broken abruptly into valleys (sic) of indescribable fertility and grandeur.— The climate is so mild that myrtles of immense size twine up our cottages & roses blow in the open air in winter.—In addition to these is the sea, which dashes against a rocky and caverned shore, presenting an ever changing scene."

But writers were not alone in their enjoyment of the contemporary taste for the Picturesque. Painters were equally enraptured, amongst whom the finest must be Samuel Palmer (1805-1881) who was much inspired by the scenery of Devon, both in the north of the county and on the fringes of Dartmoor. During the mid-1830s he had searched to find another potent *genius loci* to replace the exaltation he had experienced at Shoreham in Kent. Between 1834 and 1859 he made at least four trips and his letters reveal his delight in "dear spongy Devonshire". "Woods and woody hills must be juicy and rich," he wrote from Clovelly in 1849, but his water-colour of a wooded Exmoor valley (see opposite) is thought to have been made on his first Devon visit fifteen years before. It is inscribed "From Castle Hotel Linton D. N. Devon." and "rather young Trees/ but with the dark hollows/—stems—Nightingale."

The work was painted from the terrace of a still existing hotel. It is one of several North Devon studies that Palmer painted at this time, and if it lacks the incandescence of his earlier work, the authenticity of this quietly enraptured study makes it one of the most beautiful of the Devonshire landscapes ever to have been painted.

CLOVELLY

According to Thomas Westcote's *View of Devonshire* (c.1630), Clovelly had for centuries been a small fishing village, noted for its herrings. His observation was recorded soon after George Cary (1543-1601), a Middle Temple lawyer and Sheriff of Devon, had built in 1587 the massive pier so much in evidence at Clovelly today. On either side of its fragile harbour—the only safe one between Appledore and Boscastle—are tremendous hanging cliffs, with long and thickly wooded slopes.

Until the middle of the nineteenth century, Clovelly remained unknown outside its immediate vicinity. Yet after 1855 and the publication of *Westward Ho!*, all this was to change. Charles Kingsley, a Devon-born writer, knew the district well: he came to Clovelly when he was twelve, his father having been appointed rector here. Clovelly and the Carys both feature in the novel, as do Richard Grenville and Robert Yeo, the latter based on a former landlord of The Red Lion. Kingsley best sums up the village himself: "It is as the place had stood still while all the world had been rushing and rumbling past it."

In the late nineteenth century, Kingsley's son-in-law, the Reverend William Harrison, then rector of Clovelly, wrote about the time before the book's success: "Those were the prehistoric days of silence and solitude, when the life of the place went on undisturbed and untroubled by the big world around. It is very different now—

at any rate for six months of the year. There are days when the little village is like a fair; when the visitors arrive in troops and battalions, by sea and land, and with frank simplicity of mind take all possible pains to destroy the sense of beauty and repose and quiet which they are supposed to value and seek." Tourism, if not yet mass tourism, was replacing the old ways of earning a living. Yet, in spite of these inundations, Clovelly has

Clovelly's steeply rising, cobbled street.

somehow managed to 'survive' unchanged. This is largely as a result of the efforts of Christine Hamlyn, who 'preserved' the village as it can be seen today: quaint and picturesque but attractive in its own artificial way.

The print of Clovelly Bay (above) is an engraving of an oil by J.M.W. Turner, in the collection of The National Gallery of Ireland. The scene was painted at Buck's Mills, and looks towards Clovelly and Hartland Point.

Turner had a number of connections with Devon: his father, a barber, was born in South Molton, his uncles lived in Exeter and Barnstaple (he called on both on his 1811 tour) and he visited the county on three extensive tours which produced about 30 finished watercolours, at least five large oils and fifteen oil sketches of Devon subjects. Amongst these is his early masterpiece *Crossing the Brook* (1815) based on studies made in and around the Tamar valley including Gunnislake Bridge.

'Clovelly Bay', an engraving by W. Miller
after an oil painting by Turner, c.1823

DARTMOOR

Devon has a highly complex geology: granite blocks on Dartmoor

Dartmoor, the gently undulated wilderness in the rough centre of the county, covers an area of 365 square miles and rises to a height, at Yes Tor and High Willhays, of over 2,000 feet. Here, at least on occasion, the mist descends, the rain drives, the wind moans over heather and golden furze, the trees are sculpted by the prevailing winds and the wayfarer can be defeated by the black sponge of the peat beds which cover large areas of the moor. But at other times, in another disposition, when in the sunlight the quick wing beat of a flushed skylark rises exultant above the silken grass, the landscape can take on a more beneficent mood. There comes a sense of freedom, purity, and calm; the fevered life of the city seems at that moment worthless and remote. Even the timeless granite tors take on something of the domesticity of the Mappin Terraces at the London Zoo. But do not to be deceived! Devonshire is a gentle countryside but at its heart lies a wilderness, bleak, unforgiving and remote.

There are fine books on Dartmoor by, amongst others, William Crossing (1909) and R. Hansford Worth (1953), but the way to know it, to live and breathe it, is to walk it—and to walk deep within and across it, ideally for days at a time. For ten days last September I undertook such a walk. Sleeping under the stars, I learnt from first-hand experience how deep the wind can cut, the rain can drench, the feet can struggle to manoeuvre rocks, puddles, tufts and sphagnum bogs. At the same time I discovered the exhilaration that comes from living in the midst of one of the most beautiful places on earth.

Apart from the granite, scattered as rocks and piled into fleshy tors, water is the moor's predominant element. At all times the ground is squelchy, and fast-running streams and rivers abound; of the West Devonshire rivers only the Tamar, the Exe, the Torridge, the East Dean and the Exmoor rivers rise elsewhere. In this naked boggy landscape a timeless world of silence suggests that the moor has always been remote from human concern.

But this is far from true. Humans have occupied Dartmoor since at least 4000 B.C. The first stone huts were not erected and the land divided into territories until around 1500 B.C. This initial settlement was followed by Iron Age hillforts erected on the edge of the moor around 600 B.C.

From the middle of the twelfth century, rich deposits of tin-ore have been worked on Dartmoor: Lydford, Tavistock, Chagford and Ashburton were stannary towns to which those who mined the metal had to take their findings to be weighed and stamped. In the eighteenth century, vertical shafts were dug, and lead, copper, iron and arsenic were also mined. And still active are the china clay pits at Lee Moor (see page 42) but, arguably, Dartmoor's heaviest money-maker is now tourism, which began during the last century when hotels were opened in Chagford and Moretonhampstead.

A sheephole in a field on Dartmoor, near Dartmeet.

EXMOOR

Much of the beauty of Exmoor lies in the diversity of its landscape. The magnificent thirty-five miles of coastline with some of the highest cliffs in the country; the great sweeps of heather and bracken moorland; the deep valleys and combes, lush and thickly wooded with tumbling streams rushing to the coast, and not least the ancient oak woodlands, make it one of the most beautiful, inimitable and fascinating areas of Britain to explore.

Compared to Dartmoor, the high and undulating plateau of Exmoor—the second smallest National Park in England and Wales—is less forbidding and barren. But areas of wild countryside do remain in its central heartland; these include The Chains, Exe Plain and the Upper Badgworthy valley, roughly corresponding to the old Exmoor Forest, never wooded but used in mediæval times as an open hunting ground. A few years ago, in exceptionally heavy rain and wind, I walked The Chains, a six-mile stretch of open moorland over 1,500 feet high where many of Exmoor's streams—the Exe, Barle and West Lyn—rise in its boggy heartland. It was an exhausting undertaking. But then on clear days up on the brackeny heights with views across the shining waters of the Bristol Channel, nowhere on earth can feel more relaxing, more peaceful and, as some of its early nineteenth-century visitors (Shelley amongst them) described it, more sublime.

More than 30 miles across from east to west and nearly 20 miles from north to south at its widest point, Exmoor is an area of smoothly moulded hills, reaching a surprisingly constant height of about 1,200 feet. Of its approximately 265 square miles, about two-thirds lie in west Somerset and the remaining third in Devon. The county border splits Exmoor just at the point where the wild Doones supposedly rampaged in the area around Lank Combe, on the west bank of Badgworthy Water. But this is not the only Devon place that receives a mention in R.D. Blackmore's *Lorna Doone*, published in 1869.

Of the history of Exmoor there is relatively little of outstanding importance. For most of its time, apart from the valleys and lower lying fringes, it has been largely uninhabited and there are few outstanding physical remains. Its prehistoric monuments—round barrows, stone circles, enclosures and hill forts—number many scores but are less extensive than those on Dartmoor. The Romans also left little trace, apart from two small coastal forts; and the so-called Dark Ages are chiefly represented by the Caractacus stone on Winsford Hill in Somerset. The main impact of the Norman conquest was the imposition of forest law in the central heartland, an area in which the king had sole hunting rights. Coupled with the climate and remoteness of the area,

the latter effectively preserved the moor's wilderness until the nineteenth century.

In 1818, 10,000 acres of the former forest lands were purchased by a Worcestershire industrialist, John Knight, who attempted to develop Exmoor as a profitable agricultural community. He and his son reclaimed many acres of barren moorland, constructed roads, built farms, inaugurated drainage schemes and planted beech trees as windbreaks, but their efforts, if partially successful, remain important today if only because they are largely responsible for much of Exmoor's present landscape pattern.

Exmoor: view from Martinhoe towards Slattenslade.

CHAPTER TWO:

Animal, Vegetable, Mineral

Landscape plotted and pieced—fold, fallow and plough;
And all trades, their gear and tackle and trim.
All things counter, original, spare, strange;
Whatever is fickle, freckled (who knows how?)

Gerard Manley Hopkins, 1868

Rainbow, trees and sheep near Bondleigh, North Tawton.

DEVONSHIRE RAIN

As the fashion for sea bathing and villas with maritime views grew, the fishing villages and small towns of the Devon coast became popular with summer visitors. Jane Austen and her parents tried Sidmouth in 1801, and Dawlish and Teignmouth in 1802. Another visitor to Teignmouth was the poet John Keats, who was there in 1818. The weather was abnormally wet for the whole month of March, and he treated it to splendid invective:

"It is a splashy, rainy, misty, snowy, foggy, haily, floody, muddy, slipshod County—the hills are very beautiful, when you get a sight of 'em—the Primroses are out, but then you are in—the Cliffs are of a fine deep colour, but then the Clouds are continually vieing with them."

And on Saturday 14th March he wrote to his friend John Hamilton Reynolds:

"Being agog to see some Devonshire, I would have taken a walk the first day, but the rain would not let me; and the second, but the rain would not let me; and the third, but the rain forbade it—Ditto 4—Ditto 5—ditto—So I made up my mind to stop in doors, and catch a sight between the showers; and behold I saw a pretty valley—pretty cliffs, pretty Brooks, pretty Meadows, pretty trees, both standing as they were created, and blown down as they are uncreated—The green is beautiful, as they say, and the pity is that it is amphibious—

mais! but alas! the flowers here wait as naturally for the Rain twice a day as the Muscles do for the Tide,—so we look upon a brook in these parts as you look upon a Dash in your Country—there must be something to support this, aye, fog, hail, snow, rain, Mist—blanketing up three parts of the year—This Devonshire is like Lydia Languish, very entertaining when at smiles, but cursedly subject to sympathetic moisture."

Rain on Dartmoor, near Hound Tor.

Devon rain at its heaviest.: mourners outside St. James the Less, Huish, at the funeral of the Hon. Mark Rolle in 1907.

DARTMOOR PONIES

Dartmoor, as everyone knows, is the home ground of one of Devon's most famous breeds: the Dartmoor pony. But just as the moor is often shrouded in mist, so is their early history.

The earliest evidence for the existence of ponies on Dartmoor is hoofprints discovered on Shaugh Moor which date back to around 2000 B.C. As the hoofprints were within the boundaries of a Bronze age settlement, it is assumed they are those of domesticated animals.

There is however only uncertain evidence that ponies existed on the moor before the arrival of the Romans in 55 B.C. More certain is that the original stock was introduced by the Saxon invaders who after 614 set about the systematic conquest of Devon. After 658, they occupied some of the richest lands in the county; by 682 the Saxon king Centwine had driven the British "as far as the sea". We do not know where his decisive battle was fought, but it was probably in mid-Devon, to the north of Dartmoor. With this battle, most of Devon, if not all, passed into Saxon hands, and the ancient British kingdom of Dumnonia shrank to what is now the county of Cornwall. The invaders were great farmers who, it is virtually certain, brought their livestock with them. We can therefore assume that the Dartmoor pony (*Equus caballus*) is the descendant

of the little horses that hauled their wooden farm carts. In support of this, there is a reference in the will of the Saxon bishop Aelfwold of Crediton (997-1012) who left "to the atheling forty mancuses of gold

Dartmoor ponies near the Merrivale stone row, towards Tavistock.

and the wild horses on the land of Ashburton". The Ashburton estate then stretched well into the moor, and there can be little doubt that his "wild horses" were related to the ancestors of the present animals.

Whatever the facts as to its origin in Devon, the contemporary Dartmoor pony has certainly been the result of evolution by natural selection under conditions of exceptional harshness: eighty-two inches of average rainfall, a general lack of shelter from the wind and rain, and of lush herbage, creating an environment as wet and wild as any other in the British Isles. Such conditions have moulded its sturdy, independent character, built its tough physique and even determined its size. Yet a pony on Dartmoor is not necessarily of the Dartmoor breed; others such as Shetland and Arab have been introduced at various times.

The ponies on the moor are not wild animals. Although left to run across its 365 square miles, they are all owned. Farmers mark their ponies by branding their coats, making cuts in their ears, cutting tail hair or by a combination of these methods. Nevertheless, although certain farms on Dartmoor have rights to graze a specific number of cattle, sheep and ponies on particular moorland areas—the commons—the vast majority of ponies are untamed in that they are neither trained, ridden or handled by people.

They live out on the moor all year round, spending most of their time in small herds of mares with one adult stallion and young ponies. In late September and early October the pony drifts are held. At these, the ponies are rounded up, separated into groups according to ownership and the foals of the year branded with their owners' marks.

In 1950 there were approximately 30,000 ponies on the moor; today there are fewer than 3,000.

A lone Dartmoor pony.

GREAT TREES

With its warm and rainy climate, the Devon landscape has never suffered from a shortage of trees; rather the reverse. In fact at one time it consisted of almost nothing else: uncolonised stretches of woodland—mile upon mile of undulant tree-tops and an almost impenetrable interior. Even as late as Domesday, when the county's total population was no more than 60,000 to 80,000 people, forests predominated almost everywhere. Yet on the eve of the Black Death, Devon was already a very different kind of landscape; all over the county the virgin woods had been felled; the cleared areas were more conspicuous than the uncleared. And so the felling has continued, century after century, and often at an alarming rate. Nonetheless one can be surprised by the extent of woodland that exists and, too, the number of isolated but not always treasured specimens.

Trees of this magnificence are, of course, still a relatively common feature of the Devon landscape. Amongst the most spectacular are the Turkey Oak at Knighthayes Court (a so-called National Champion), the ancient Yew in the churchyard of South Brent, a Monkey Puzzle at Bicton (also a Champion Tree, namely one of the biggest of its type in the country), a mighty Sitka Spruce at Castlehill, an enormous oak at Sticklepath, and the Meavy Oak in which, it is said, nine people once dined. There are also, of course, the oaks of

Wistman's Wood on Dartmoor.

But if only because of its close association with the county, pride of place might be given to the the sub-evergreen Lucombe oak (*Quercus x hispanica 'Lucombeana'*). This was raised by a Mr. Lucombe, an Exeter nurseryman, from seeds of trees of his own growth planted in 1762. When these began to grow he noticed with his gardener's eye that one amongst them retained its leaves throughout the winter. This tree he propagated by grafting.

When the original was twenty years old and about three feet in circumference, Mr Lucombe had it cut down for the purpose of making his coffin. Nonetheless,

The Lucombe Oak at Phear Park, Exmouth.

so the story goes, he lived much longer than he had anticipated so he then decided to fell a larger and much older tree. This he had sawn into planks and stored under his bed in readiness for his death. And, as J.C. Loudon writes in *Arboretum et Fruticetum Britannicum* of 1838, "inside these planks, on which for many years he had reposed, he was at last put to rest, at the advanced age of 102 years."

The finest Devon specimen of a Lucombe oak is at Phear Park in Exmouth; in 1990 it measured 25 cm by 242 cm. Fine specimens are also to be seen in the vicinity of Reed Hall, Exeter.

Wistman's Wood, north of Two Bridges, Dartmoor.

THE DEVON LANE

A Devon lane. Detail of painting by Ben Hartley (1933-1996), probably of Westlake, near Ermington, where he lived for twenty-three years.

In spring the Devon lanes are vibrant with the loveliest of flowers—first snowdrops, blackthorn and the early primroses, followed from late April to early June by bluebells, wood anemones, campions, yellow archangels, early purple orchids and hawthorn. As summer progresses, these are followed by dog roses, cow parsley, honeysuckle, meadow sweet, and the piercing mauvy-blue flowers of vetch—all of which the Devon parson, W. Keble Martin, depicted in colour in his book *The Concise British Flora* (see also page 87).

Hedgerows are known to support a tremendous range of other wildlife: over 600 plant species, 1500 insects, 65 birds and 20 mammal species have been recorded at some time living or feeding in the Devonshire hedgerows. At least 30 species of birds actually nest in them, too. Half our native mammals—mice, voles, shrews, stoats, weasels, rabbits, foxes and badgers—make their homes in hedges. It has been estimated that of Devon's 73 non-woodland trees, more than half a million isolated trees are to be found in her hedges, banks and walls.

In fact hedges have shaped and defined the character of the Devon countryside for centuries. The hedgerow network can be dated back 7,000 years, when farming first started in Britain. Some hedges—like those originally belonging to the earthworks of hill forts—are as much as 4,000 years old; yet others, conserving ancient land boundaries, can be dated from the Bronze Age. Only prehistoric and Roman remains, which are rare in Devon, are older than many of its common hedges. It is for this reason that many archæologists have asserted that the hedgerow system is not only Devon's biggest and most magnificent prehistoric monument but the only one to have remained virtually intact until the middle of this century.

W.G. Hoskins has suggested that at least a quarter of the county's hedges are more than 800 years old. But the period between 1150 and 1350, one of exceptional colonisation of the Devon countryside, was when most of the county's small irregular fields, winding sunken lanes and boundary banks came into being. Estimates carried out in 1841 put the stock of Devon's hedges at that time as between 50,000 and 60,000 miles. Although there has subsequently been a great deal of hedge removal (more than 150,000 miles of British hedgerow have been grubbed up since 1945), the hedge remains the most prominent and characteristic feature of the present-day Devon landscape.

A Devon lane near East Budleigh and Hayes Barton, where Raleigh was born in 1552.

SOME DEVONSHIRE GARDENS

Devon is fortunate in the number of its fine gardens. Amongst these can be included those at Knighthayes Court near Tiverton; Killerton House, Broad Clyst, near Exeter; Tapeley Park, near Instow; the Royal Horticultural garden at Rosemoor, near Torrington; Coleton Fishacre, near Kingswear; Dartington Hall, near Totnes and The Garden House, near Yelverton. It is the last three that are described here.

They were all created by exceptional individuals, largely between and after the two Great World Wars. Coleton Fishacre, a 20-acre garden set within a typical Devon combe sloping down to the cliff tops and the sea, was created by Rupert and Lady Dorothy D'Oyly Carte after their Arts and Crafts style house had been completed in 1926. Dartington Hall, a 21-acre landscape garden adjacent to and complementing a grey stone mediæval building (see page 73), was largely created by Dorothy Elmhirst from the mid-1920s onwards; and the eight-acre Garden House, lying on the north-facing slope of a quiet valley running down to the River Tavy, was begun by Katherine and Lionel Fortescue after 1945. The situation and character of these places could not be more different. Coleton, which relies on its seclusion and exceptional mildness of climate, is characterised by

the planting of large numbers of rhododendrons, camellias and other trees and shrubs from different countries, many seldom seen growing outside in the British Isles. But this is not all. Providing a transition between the house and the woodland area that slopes beneath it are a series of formal terraced areas of subtle design. The view, framed by pines, of Pudcombe Cove with the Eastern Black Rock out to sea (which can be viewed from the so-called Gazebo), is also astonishingly successful; without it the garden would lose much of its understated charm.

The character of the garden at Dartington Hall is very different. Whereas Coleton Fishacre, a long narrow

A water feature in the Rill Garden at Coleton Fishacre, near Kingswear.

garden enclosed by valley sides, is wooded with a thick tree canopy, the former is primarily an open space with its so-called Tiltyard an empty green sward at its heart. And if the former contains a great number of relatively recently planted species, the latter depends on a centuries-old fabric of buildings and fine old trees: great Planes, a monumental Turkey oak and a celebrated row of Sweet Chestnuts, not less than 400 years old, add grandeur to the slightly formal but nonetheless inimitable nobility of the place. There is, too, yet another difference between Dartington and both Coleton Fishacre and The Garden House. Whereas both the latter were laid out for the private pleasure of their respective owners, the Dartington garden was from the start conceived for public delight.

The spirit of The Garden House is different again: much of it is either enclosed or compartmentalised, and the low planting is both crowded and intense; the mood reminiscent of Sissinghurst, but without the poetry and sense of style at Dartington. There are small lawns, walls and structural hedges but the atmosphere is intimate and almost tapestried; the garden depends on the wide range of colourful planting (there are over 6000 different varieties planted here) peaking in the two-acre walled garden in July when the Sidalceas, Astilbes and Dieramas are at their best.

View toward the church of St. Andrew's, Buckland Monachorum, from the Top Garden of The Garden House.

THE LUSTLEIGH ORCHARD

Lustleigh, on the eastern edge of Dartmoor, is a granite village of thatched cottages invaded by modern residences; three-quarters of its current inhabitants are retired people, and almost everyone an 'incomer'. The scattered village, originally a grouping of farms and farm buildings, clusters around the thirteenth-century church. Its font is Norman and its churchyard resembles the shape of a very early religious site. Yet if the origins of the cider orchard immediately adjacent to the village are not known, it is certainly very old—its preservation largely due to the fact that the area is littered with sizeable granite boulders. Just over four acres in extent, since 1960 it has been owned by the parish, and remains a permanent site for its May Day Festival.

According to Barry Sessions—an oyster farmer, Rescue Team instructor and Parish Counsellor who has cared for the orchard as a labour of love for fifteen out of the twenty years he has lived in the village—the oldest trees are about ninety years of age. Yet, he told me, new ones are continuously replacing those that have died, some in memory of those who had played in the orchard as children.

On the day of my visit towards the end of April, the apple trees, coral pink and white, were in full flower; the sun was shining and in a space amongst the trees a stately Maypole, wrapped in shining ribbons, had been erected in preparation for the forthcoming celebration. As we sat amongst the boulders, Barry Sessions recounted how this ancient pagan expression of joy at the beginning of true summer had once been held in the sloping valley-side woods above the village.

Whether the Maypole was a permanent fixture, a tree dragged in from the wood by oxen with flower-tipped horns or a living tree stuck full of flags or ribbons, we shall never know, nor for how long Mayday has been celebrated in this valley. Nonetheless, we can appreciate why garlands are carried by children, why a bonfire is lit, why carols have been sung on towers, why the May Queen is still crowned with flowers (at Lustleigh her name is also carved into a monumental boulder), why villagers once spent the night in the woods and carried back green branches in the morning— because, of course, of our innate and natural joy at the return of life to the cold earth.

But the Puritans thought otherwise; for them Mayday was more a sacrilege than the celebration of returning life. Recognising many of these customs for the fertility rites that they undoubtedly were, they sought to put them down. The indictment of Philip Stubbes in his *Anatomie of Abuses* of 1583 is well

known. He writes about a "great Lord present amongst them, as superintendent and Lord over their pastimes and sportes, namely, Sathan, prince of hel." But what is less well known is that the highest Maypole in history disappeared in 1717, when Sir Isaac Newton removed it to support what was in his time the most powerful telescope in the world. The modern age can be dated from that year.

Lustleigh town orchard: apple trees in flower towards the end of April.

LEE MOOR CLAY WORKS

Considering its wild, inhospitable character, Dartmoor has been the centre of a surprising amount of industrial activity. Although tin working, the mining of copper, silver, lead and zinc, the making of gunpowder and the quarrying of granite have been carried out for centuries, china clay extraction is the only activity to have grown in this century.

China clay, or kaolin, is decomposed felspar, a component of granite. The decomposition or kaolinisation is caused by the aciditic action of the hot volcanic gases and liquids being forced up through the granite by extreme pressure of heat. The action took place millions of years ago, and the process lasted for thousands of years.

Originally, extraction involved mixing the clay with water, which was passed over a series of mica traps; the heavier sand settled out, allowing the clay-water to flow on. Modern methods continue to depend on the extensive use of water power. The clay is washed from the pit by high pressure hoses and the resulting material pumped from the pit to a sand separation plant where the coarse sand is removed. The remaining clay and water mixture is then treated to remove the fine sand and mica before the clay is dried.

The Lee Moor Clay Works (north-east of Plymouth) were opened in 1830 when John Dickens, in partnership with John Cowley, a naval officer from Plymouth, leased the clay-bearing land at Lee Moor from the Earl of Morley on a twenty-one year lease. In 1919 a new company, English China Clays, was formed by the amalgamation of three small companies. Yet in spite of the fact that at that time the Lee Moor pit was the largest in the county, the output from Devon as a whole has always been a fraction of that from Cornwall: from 1900 to 1943 it was only about one-tenth. Most of the clay, produced in several grades, is exported from Plymouth; these include a high-grade coating clay, filler-grade clays, a potting clay and two calcined clays. The material has numerous uses, including papermaking and ceramics; rubber, paints, textiles, inks, dyes, some soaps and most toothpastes.

To visit the vast, unearthly, Lee Moor site is a singular experience. The pits area, some 500 acres in extent, is a moon-landscape: it is whiteish in colour, composed of gigantic craters, milky aquamarine lakes, fissure-sided tips and in one place a kind of stepped ziggurat. The bulldozers at the bottom of the huge pits look like children's toys. Pollution is undeniable. Near Plymouth the river Plym flows almost milk-white with the washings of the clay, whilst near Kingsteignton the small leaves of the spring hedges are soon powdered with white dust. Nonetheless the greyish white mounds of waste 'sand'

have created a silent, desolate yet imposing beauty of their own own. There is a rare point, as the agricultural writer Arthur Young (1741-1820) saw, when industrial ugliness can become sublime.

China clay working at Lee Moor, near Shaugh Prior.

43

CHAPTER THREE:

Place

In the quiet early sunny morning it seemed to me as if that place must be one of the loveliest nooks in the Paradise of this world.

Francis Kilvert, 1871-4

The stone row at Drizzlecombe, near Sheepstor, south Dartmoor.

EXETER

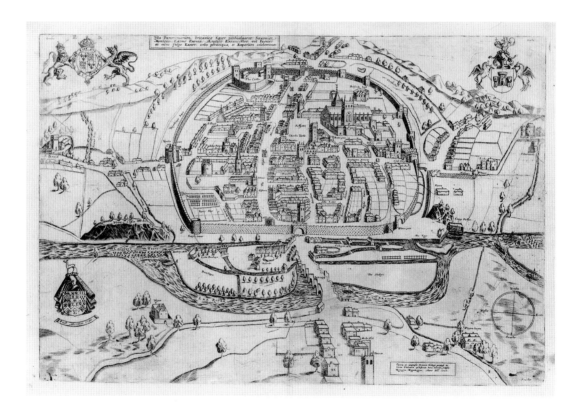

Exeter, with a population of slightly more than 100,000 people, is one of the historic cities of England. The Romans gave it its essential character; they laid down its central crossing at North and South streets, and built the city wall which later provided protection from the Danes. Since 1050 the city has been the seat of a bishop and of a cathedral (see pages 71 and 96). Since 1080 the city has had a (Norman) castle, and in

John Hooker's map of Exeter, drawn in A.D. 1587.
The original belongs to Exeter City Museums.

the twelfth century it gained a Guildhall. Thereafter it grew in prosperity and population. By the time when John Hooker's map was drawn in 1587, Exeter was one of the most important cities in England. From the fifteenth century it was also one of the chief cloth markets of the South-West. Yet, as we can see from a perusal of Hooker's map on the previous page, it was then small in extent: a person could walk around the entire circuit of its walls (some one and a half miles in length) in a matter of minutes. In it we can see the High Street, the Cathedral with its two Norman towers, the Bishop's Palace, the Castle, eleven parish churches, the mediæval bridge over the Exe, three gates in the city walls and, prominently, the city walls themselves.

W.G. Hoskins has calculated that in the last quarter of the sixteenth century, when the city's total population was between nine and ten thousand—about two thousand families at the most—Exeter had about a hundred merchants. These covered the whole range of trading, from direct import from overseas or London and the coastal ports, down to pennyworths of things sold on the premises.

The grandest of their houses could be very comfortable—at that time the richest merchant was worth ten times as much as the smallest. Nonetheless, the majority of Exeter's citizens lived less affluently and in far more crowded conditions: in narrow, congested streets whose teeming life and womb-like security was only opened up in the eighteenth century when ambitious new residential developments were built outside the walls. The city's Georgian terraces and crescents,

though savagely depleted, remain an engaging example of the civic benefits of subjecting individualism to the interests of neighbourly decorum.

Although Exeter's mediæval centre was substantially destroyed during the war in 1942, the majority of its civic buildings, including the cathedral and the exquisite houses around its green, still survive. Sadly, but characteristically, postwar Exeter does not live up to their example: like the postwar cities of Leicester, Worcester and Salisbury, the vandalism of weak architecture married to an overwhelming consumerism have bequeathed to us a city architecturally mediocre in its twentieth-century parts.

Houses on the north side of Cathedral Close, Exeter. The building on the left is now The Devon and Exeter Institution.

BIDEFORD

'A View of Bideford from Upcott Hill', painted by an anonymous artist.
The original is in the Burton Art Gallery and Museum, Bideford.

There have been many Bidefords, one of North Devon's most attractive towns. The first was a settlement of people living on the edge of marshland on the west bank of the Torridge where it begins to widen into its estuary. The second existed in the last quarter of the thirteenth century, by which time there was a wooden bridge joining river bank to river bank and a market and five-day fair. The third was in Elizabethan times: by 1573 the town had grown sufficiently to receive a charter of incorporation from the Queen. At that time Sir Richard Grenville's colonisation of Virginia and Carolina had led to the establishment of considerable American trade. At the end of the seventeenth century and the first quarter of the eighteenth, shipbuilding and imported tobacco were bringing unprecedented prosperity to the growing town.

It was at that time that the handsome brick houses still standing in Bridgeland Street (c.1690-1700) were built. Daniel Defoe, who visited at the time, called this street "well inhabited by considerable and wealthy merchants who trade to most parts of the trading world." He also admired Bideford as a whole; it was, he wrote, a "pleasant, clean, well-built town… The more ancient street, which lies next the river, is very pleasant, where is the bridge, a very noble quay, and the custom-house. This part is very well built and populous, and fronts the river above three-quarters of a mile."

But Bideford's early eighteenth-century prosperity was short lived. In the following decades one after another of the town's overseas trades collapsed, and by the end of the nineteenth century only a coasting trade remained. In 1801 its population was down to just under 3,000 people. By 1901 it had risen to 8,754. Now it is more than 12,000.

The painting on the previous page shows Bideford in its fifth manifestation: a small, quiet, untroubled place nestling in a vast landscape. Maybe at that time— the mid-nineteenth century—the town enjoyed little prosperity and none of the excitement of bustling nineteenth-century Plymouth, but its scale and pace were appropriate to a desirable human norm. It remains enjoyable today: less ugly than modern Barnstaple, less congested than Plymouth, both of which have lost their souls to shopping; less go-ahead, even melancholy in its by-passed status, but convivial nonetheless. With its broad quay fronting the fast-flowing tidal river, streets of white-painted houses climbing steeply up the hillside which slopes up from the Torridge, and a handsome stone bridge joining the town to East-the-Water on the opposite bank, it remains a pleasure to visit and live in. The river is a continuous and lively delight; there are pleasant streets and passages of small white-walled houses, interesting quayside activities, an attractive park and good Art Gallery. All it needs is a sensitive Prince to bring this economic Sleeping Beauty to greater life.

Bideford Long Bridge over the Torridge.
It has twenty-four irregularly spaced arches.

TORQUAY

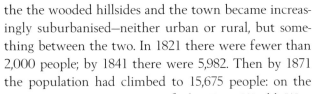

'Tor' means 'high craggy hill' and Torquay, like Rome, is built on seven of these. Three of them—Waldon, Braddons and Park Hill—rise steeply from the inner harbour and give it shelter from the north and east winds. The place was once a small farming and fishing community, and the quay where the fish were landed lay at the mouth of the Fleet, a river which ran through a meadow and gave way to mud flats as it reached the sea. Access was gained through two valleys now known as Fleet Street (under which the river runs) and Torwood Street, now both lined with shops.

Later, the town absorbed the ancient parishes of Cockington, Tor Mohun and St. Marychurch. But with the coming of the nineteenth century, the old pattern of rural and seafaring life was replaced by the idea of Torquay as a fashionable resort. The mild winter climate, the superb natural position and the supposed benefits of sea bathing, combined to attract growing numbers; before long elegant villas began to appear on the the wooded hillsides and the town became increasingly suburbanised—neither urban or rural, but something between the two. In 1821 there were fewer than 2,000 people; by 1841 there were 5,982. Then by 1871 the population had climbed to 15,675 people: on the eve of the First World War, Torquay had swollen to 40,000. It now stands at about 121,000.

With its wooded drives and terraces following the contours of the hills, inner Torquay remains a predominantly mid-Victorian town—and much of it a pleasing one. The hilly area east of the harbour with its stylish stuccoed Italianate villas is especially attractive. Here is Hesketh Crescent of the 1840s, a lovely (if slightly coarse) cream-coloured, Georgian-style set-piece, facing Tor Bay which on a luminous day, with its surrounding palms and yuccas, can be reminiscent of the south of France.

But in this century, Torquay changed; it has become a popular holiday and retirement centre. With its

The view of Tor Bay from Hesketh Crescent, Torquay.

temperate winters, its harbour bobbing with pleasure boats, its sands peopled with basking sun-lovers, its streets congested with chain-store shops and all the amenities of a modern holiday resort, it has lost much of its exclusive Victorian and Edwardian flavour. It is now congested with traffic, with often dullish shops and 'leisure' opportunities designed for tourists with little to do but relax in the sun or spend their money. But, like Sydney, in spite of everything Torquay continues to occupy a superb position (on the north promontory of Tor Bay), and to have a lingering historic charm.

'A View of Torquay' by John Rawson Walker, c.1850.
The original is in the collection of Torre Abbey.

TOTNES

Hoskins calls it, next to Exeter and Plymouth, the most interesting town in Devon: a lively little place on a hill rising from the west bank of the river Dart. Writing over two hundred years earlier, Daniel Defoe called it "a very good town to live in", and even Pevsner, rarely fulsome, rises to effusion when he described Totnes as "one of the most rewarding small towns in England". I agree with all their judgements.

It is an ancient settlement. A *burh* very probably existed here from about the middle of the tenth century, but it does not appear in historical records until the reign of Edgar (958-75). After the Norman conquest the town spread down its main artery to the river Dart.

Like other Devon towns, its wealth grew from cloth, leather and farming, combined with the advantages of the navigable Dart estuary. By Henry VIII's time it was second only to Exeter in merchant-wealth and ranked fifteenth among all English provincial towns. This prosperity lasted from the fifteenth to the mid-seventeenth century, when many of the houses along Fore Street and the High Street were entirely rebuilt.

But from the mid-seventeenth century the merchant community declined and the town began to rely on its strength as a local market centre; thereafter the population grew only slowly. The Totnes of today, its centre barely scathed by post-war 'development' has an almost archetypal form: a close-knit texture of small buildings and narrow streets: a working port; a Norman castle on a hump-backed mound; a Tudor Guildhall; its main street lined by beautiful merchant's houses and, in the centre of it all, a handsome fifteenth-century parish and priory church.

Within a stone's throw of the latter's handsome tower resides Bill Bennett, who has lived here since 1941, when he came as a thirteen-year-old fleeing with his family from the blitz on Plymouth where he was born. Now in energetic retirement, Bill's fidelity towards the town of which he has been Mayor three times—in 1969, 1977 and 1996—is vividly clear to all who know him. "Oh! yes, I've seen such changes here," he exclaims with a mixture of pride and astonishment. "In my time, Totnes, which for at least a decade after the Second World War was filled with long-established family businesses, has become in some ways a different and less personal kind of place. The three secondary schools have joined to form one large comprehensive. More recently, the old Broomborough and Cottage Hospitals have been razed and a new Community Hospital has been built in their stead. The arrival of two supermarkets has affected many small local businesses; they may retain their family name but are now run by new owners. At the same time, council estates and private housing have

raised the population to 7,250. Reeves' Timber and Harris's Bacon factory have also closed but perhaps the biggest change was in 1974 when the most ancient Borough of Totnes was demoted to Parish Council status, with all the major decisions henceforth made by the District and County Councils. Yet, believe me, some of the changes affecting our town have been for the good. Totnes used to be a more close-knit community than it is today but it was run by a small and tight-knit social hierarchy of local landowners, the vicar, the headmaster and the like; today it's benefited by a wider range of people having more say in its future. And despite the threat of an increase of population which could only further weaken the feeling of intimacy which characterises the town, Totnes remains a marvellous, caring and vibrant place in which to live. It retains a consciousness of calm and history; a living sense of a community without either the extremes of poverty or wealth. It enters the millennium with confidence and pride. *Vivat floreat Totnesia."*

Totnes, from Bridgetown. The view looks across the town, towards the castle and St. Mary's church.

PLYMOUTH

*A view towards the Gateway of the Royal William Victualling
Yard, Stonehouse, surmounted by its statue of William IV.*

54

Plymouth is an acquired taste. It is a sprawling megalopolis of almost a quarter of a million people, the ninth biggest in England and by far the largest and most urban of Devonshire's numerous settlements (its population was nearly 242,000 in 1991). But in spite of its position and prodigious history, for more than a quarter of a century I found little pleasure in it. I saw soulless housing (like that of the North Prospect Estate), dismally ugly suburbs and a city centre as dull and heartless as any I had ever known. Bombing had devastated much of this central area (3,754 houses destroyed, 68,348 damaged), but the planning that went forwards in its wake was another lost opportunity. In addition to this post-war desolation, the city suffers from two further disablements: an historic introversion and the present loss of its long-established *raison d'être*. Today, only about 4,000 people are employed where at least 25,000 had once worked in the naval dockyards. A taxi driver shared with me his despair, the poverty of his colleagues and their sense of rejection and hopelessness.

But Plymouth's character is more complicated than this. To stroll along the Hoe is to enjoy one of the finest views in Europe. Ahead, the vast expanse is alive with small toy-sized boats. To the right lies Drake's island and the wooded headland of Mount Edgcumbe. To the left, there is the Citadel, the great fortress built in 1666 by Charles II on the site of earlier strongholds. And at one's back, neat rows of Italianate Edwardian terraces, tea gardens, statuary and the elegant, striped hulk of the old Smeaton lighthouse, brought to rest here in 1882. There is something almost Claudian about this panorama, a gloriously unencumbered natural sight.

There are other aspects of Plymouth no less appealing: the Barbican, the gateways of the Royal Citadel, and Foulston's group of civic buildings at the end of Ker Street in Devonport. The latter includes the Grecian town hall, the commemorative column and the Egyptian Institution. However, possibly the grandest group of buildings is John Rennie's Royal William Victualling Yard (built 1825-33).

There are also wonderful corners—winding alleyways, hidden gardens, fine eighteenth century houses, glimpses of the water, of green hills and promontories, the distant silhouette of forts and fortifications, figureheads and statues, tucked away in corners which possess a character like something in Cruikshank or Dickens. For me, this hubbub where all is flux and discontinuity, a palimpsest of meaning and culture, one thing superimposed and obliterating another, but somehow mysteriously cohering, has become what I most enjoy about of this lively, ugly, wonderful, but sad city.

A public garden on the Hoe, Plymouth.

APPLEDORE

In complete contrast to Plymouth, Appledore is quiet, unspoilt and on a human scale. Its origins as a human settlement can be traced back to the eleventh century. By the reign of Elizabeth it was already populous, already busy with shipbuilding, salmon fishing and the like. The shipbuilding industry, which flourished especially in the eighteenth and nineteenth centuries as a result of North American trade, still survives; some 500 people work for Appledore Shipbuilders, which builds survey vessels, harbour tugs, ferries, dredgers and other vessels up to a maximum size of 10,000 tonnes deadweight. The company's predecessors, John Hinks & Son, built replicas of the Golden Hind, a Viking longship and a Roman galleon. Prior to 1800, ships were being built on the beaches between Bideford and Appledore, leaving little trace. In 1850-6 the Richmond Dry Dock was built to meet the needs of James Yeo, who sent ships built in Prince Edward Island, Canada, to Appledore for finishing.

Lying at the end of a peninsula, Appledore is one of Devon's least 'progressed'—and therefore most delightful—settlements. It is a busy working place but, being more resistant to the idolatry of economic growth than some of Devon's towns and villages, it is largely unspoilt. The compact streets of simple eighteenth- and nineteenth-century houses, enhanced by

their harmonious proportions and unexpected variety, are a delight to explore. There is Bude Street, which contains an interesting mixture of small houses originally inhabited by families of seamen and shipyard workers; Market Street, which contains more eighteenth-century houses; and Irsha Street, once the home of several boatbuilders' yards. There are also other charming streets, mixtures of terraced cottages and handsome Georgian and early Victorian houses, besides alleyways and courts. The village scene must be much as it was two hundred years ago.

It was then that Thomas Girtin (1775-1802), one

Bude Street, Appledore.

of England's finest water-colour painters, and the friend and contemporary of Turner, visited Devon. In 1797 he travelled from Weymouth to Plymouth, sketching castles, rivers and coastal views, Exeter Cathedral and Okehampton Castle, on the way. He also painted Appledore from the Instow beach on the other side of the estuary. Girtin was then in his twenty-second year and leading the way in terms of the development of the emotional expressiveness of the water-colour as a medium.

It can be presumed that Girtin's visit was occa-sioned by the patronage of a Mr. Calvert, whose Appledore-born son (1799-1883) became one of the finest engravers in the history of art. One of his works, *The Cyder Feast*, has been enlarged and reproduced on page 114 of this book. In its own rhapsodic way it sums up much of the fecund luxuriance of the Devon landscape.

The Appledore Maritime Museum, which is a model of its kind, traces the region's seafaring tradi-tion to the present day, through a wealth of exhibits, models and photographs.

Thomas Girtin's water-colour of 'Appledore, North Devon', 1798.
The original belongs to the Courtauld Galleries in London.

CORNWORTHY'S NATURAL HISTORY

In the church of Cornworthy—one of the loveliest in the county—there is a lectern upon which rests the Cornworthy Parish Book. It was compiled in 1995 by a group of parishioners as a record of their parish and contains memories, photographs and memorabilia, as well as essays on various aspects of the parish including the school, the priory, the two churches, and a delightful illustrated account of its natural history, the outcome of years of meticulous and devoted study. This was written and illustrated by a retired teacher who has lived in Cornworthy for many years. Like Gilbert White's great book on the parish of Selbourne, published in 1789, Reg Barker's study is composed of observations of the thousands of species that populate the parish. Regrettably too long to print in its entirety, with the author's kind permission I am reprinting an abridged version below.

After a few introductory paragraphs about the village, the local agricultural environment and weather, Reg Barker describes the birds which he has so intimately observed. "During the winter," he writes,

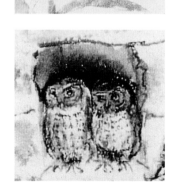

"many birds stay in the Cornworthy area, feeding along the shoreline of the Dart and the mudbanks of Bow Creek. Shelduck, Herons and other Waders can be seen on most days along the creek at low water. Jackdaws, Rooks, Carrion Crows and even Ravens winter in the area and Magpies can be seen everywhere in the village and along the hedgerows all through the year. In the sky it is always possible to see Buzzards gracefully gliding and patrolling. All the gardens host innumerable birds when food is put out for them—Collared Doves, Starlings, Tree and House Sparrows, Chaffinches, Greenfinch, Great Tits, Coal Tits and Blue Tits exploit any food available." Other local birds include Long-tailed Tits, Goldcrests, Goldfinch, Robins, Blackbirds, Thrushes, Wrens, Hedgesparrows, Great Spotted Woodpeckers and Nuthatches; but, he adds, "Unfortunately the village has a great number of domestic cats which kill many of the resident garden birds."

"… Down at Bow Creek are coppices… rich in Oak, Ash, Alder and Spruce with the occasional Spindle tree. The result of winter activity can often be detected

Little owls and a small Tortoiseshell butterfly: two water-colours by Reg Barker.

amongst the scrapings under the herbage. One can see fungi chewed, banks scoured and hazel nuts cleanly chiselled—all evidence of mice, field voles, grey squirrels and rabbits. . . Among the stunted axils of crumbling stumps are seen masses of Polypody ferns. The niches, which form naturally, are filled with leaf and bark litter and here the beautiful Tamarisk moss grows, looking like a miniature shrub. Mosses of the *Hypnum*, *Mnium*, *Brachythecium* and *Dicranella* species grow everywhere in the dark, moist areas. . . In darker spring-fed spots along the edges of the banks, Liverworts grow, their talus (flat leaves) forming dense patches. The Oak and Ash woodland is often surprisingly quiet,

but careful observation reveals a different picture—among the leaf litter there are innumerable creatures. . . such as minute Woodlice, Milli-pedes, Springtails with their long tail appendages and tiny Threadworms. . . Even smaller are the Mites which occur in their millions, seen only through a microscope."

After introducing Pheasants, Woodcock, Snipe, Sandpiper, Redshank, Stoats and Weasels, Swallows, Chiffchaffs and other birds, the author describes some of the wild flowers and grasses in the parish, of which, he tells me, he has counted 257 different species. Amongst these are Winter Heliotrope, Lesser Celandine, Hedge Bedstraw, Goosegrass, Greater and Lesser Stitchwort, Chickweed, Red Campion, Shiny Cranesbill, Little Robin, Nipplewort and Hedge Parsley. The village has many pockets of Greater Celandine, a plant noted

for its bright yellow sap, once used to cure warts. "In deep shady areas (like Corkscrew Hill and Willow Lane), there are patches of woodland where Dog's Mercury, Enchanter's Nightshade and Ramsoms (Wild Garlic) can be found." The Cornworthy Parish banks have Bluebells growing at all levels early in the year. "Where competition is not too great one can find an assortment of interesting plants and mosses like Green Alkanet, Borage, Comfrey, and the yellow Toadflax. On a drier wall one finds Pennywort, Ivy-leaved Toadflax, Field Bindweed, Red Valerian and also the pretty Crosswort Bedstraw with its lime coloured leaves and tiny axil flowers."

Thus Reg Barker introduces his record of the non-human life of only one of Devon's almost 500 parishes.

The village of Cornworthy.

HOLY WELLS

Fitz's Well, situated on the northern edge of Dartmoor, above
Okehampton and beside a pilgrim footpath that led to Canterbury.

Generations before St. Augustine landed in Britain in 597 A.D., the South-West was visited by Celtic missionaries from Ireland, Wales and Brittany; many were afterwards canonised. In fact no part of England contains so many local saints as Devon and Cornwall, which to this day contain numerous place names associated with them. In North Devon are to be found churches dedicated to Saints Helen (Abbotsham and Lundy), Brannoc (Braunton), Fili (Filleigh), Kea (Landkey), Petrock (Parracombe), Rumon (Romansleigh) and Nectan, who is remembered by two wells.

These missionaries were important because they introduced a new brand of Christianity, a holy intimacy of the human, natural and divine in vital contact with the nature-worship which prevailed during the thousand-year-old civilisation of the Celtic peoples. One especially important aspect of this worship was the veneration of water: the latter remained a strong part of the local population's spiritual beliefs and practices until the advent of Roman Christianity. It was after that time that the lore of holy wells and springs became 'christianised', and associated with the stories of particular saints. In fact the Church even managed to make use of the Celtic veneration of the severed head, which became especially potent when a skull was associated with water.

This link between the cult of the severed head and the potency of well water was preserved in the hagiography of the Celtic saints—so effectively that the mysterious beheadings of holy men quickly found a place in local folklore. In many of these stories the well is supposed to have sprung out of the ground on which the saint's head lay before it was reunited with his body.

The story of the Welsh saint Nectan is associated with this belief. One day, walking on a local beach, Nectan was attacked and decapitated by pirates. To his assassins' astonishment he bent down, picked up his head and carried it under his arm about a mile and a half inland. Here he stopped, placed the severed head on his shoulders, was instantaneously healed but lay down and died—whereupon a spring of healing water gushed out of the earth. This place is still marked by not one but two wells. The first in Stoke near Hartland; the other in nearby Welcombe, where it is sheltered by a little stone building.

There may once have been as many as 2,000 holy wells in England and another 1,200 in Wales. The recent upsurge of interest has revived a sense of their ancient sanctity, lost for centuries.

Other holy wells in Devon are to be found at Ashburton (St. Gudula's Well), Okehampton (Fitz's Well), Endsleigh, Parracombe (St. Thomas), and Ladywell, running down from South Cliff at the eastern end of the Valley of Rocks, Lynton.

The holy well of St. Nectan at Welcombe, in its own roofed enclosure to the south-east of the church.

STONE CIRCLES ON DARTMOOR

On the upland expanse of Dartmoor there is a unique assembly of prehistoric remains. Even if none of them can compare with, say, Avebury or Maiden Castle, yet because of their numbers, the wildness of their setting and great archæological interest, they remain amongst the most intriguing, beautiful and significant prehistoric antiquities in the British Isles.

There are megalithic tombs (also known as dolmens or cromlechs), standing stones or menhirs, sixty-two stone rows (also known as avenues or alignments) as well as some 1,500 hut-circles, several hundred cairns and ninety cists; but for me it is the stone circles—of which over ninety remain—which are Dartmoor's most hauntingly memorable early monuments. These were built when Egypt was young, long before the pyramids, at a time when the earliest forms of writing and numbering were being developed in the Near East, yet in winter starlight or a summer dawn they can seem as present as the hot sunshine, or a butterfly on a blade of grass.

Magical and solar symbolism, the reverence of ancestors, sacred spaces for fertility and funeral rites, calendrical devices for recording the seasons, are said to be some of the reasons why Britain's 900 prehistoric stone circles were originally constructed; but in truth (and despite a great deal of research), no one has yet established

why they were made.

On Dartmoor, the largest is Grey Wethers, north of Postbridge, two circles set side by side on the flat summit of the ridge dividing the South Teign and East Dart valleys. More accessible is Scorhill, near the village of Gidleigh, which in the early nineteenth century was described by the Reverend Samuel Rowe as "by far the finest of the rude but venerable shrines of Druidical worship in Devonshire". To walk towards it within a wide expanse of lonely country with the long ridge of Hangingstone Hill outlined in the distance, to watch the

Grey Wethers, north of Postbridge.

movement of cloud shadows passing over the tawny moor, to stand within the circle of standing stones (originally thirty-six in number but now reduced), is always a potent experience. I remember one such time in particular. One evening, sitting amongst the stones, I watched the moon's eclipse in the autumn sky. The archæologist Aubrey Burl has observed that "like many other open rings of southern England, (Scorhill) was used by several families for rituals connected with the fertility of the land." In those eerie, silent moments I discovered the yoke and power of cosmic forces upon the minds of our ancestors.

Scorhill, near Gidleigh, with the long ridge of Hangingstone Hill outlined in the far distance.

A MEDIÆVAL PULPIT

*The painted stone pulpit at St. George's,
Dittisham, with saints or apostles.*

Dittisham is a village of thatched, colour-washed houses. A visitor is led up to its golden grey church tower and then steeply down to the river Dart, shining a light silvery blue in the summery sunshine. St. George's has a Norman font, a late mediæval rood screen with painted panels and, to my eye, one of the most beautiful fifteenth-century pulpits in the county. It is made of stone (there are only sixty mediæval stone pulpits in all England, and eleven of these are in Devon; two at nearby Dartmouth and Harberton) and rests securely on a palm-like foot, also of stone. The sides of the pulpit are decorated with five canopied niches which shelter the stiffly standing figures of saints or apostles. These are separated by vertical shafts richly ornamented with bold encrusted vegetation—vine stems, their leaves and fruits as vigorous as the organic luxuriances of the local countryside. The best of Devon's indigenous art—and we can see it in this pulpit—combines a sensuous sweetness with a luxuriant magnificence, blending joy and delight with intense imaginative strength.

From a sophisticated viewpoint—and Pevsner calls the carving of the pulpit 'very crude'—the work is indeed rough, but that is its unaffected strength. It has the intense vitality of a Scottish ballad or a native folk song; the direct and immediate response to life that is found in an African mask. But the glory of the pulpit resides not only in its carving but in its colouring: crimson, white and ultramarine.

Other Devon churches have retained traces of their original colour—the stone pulpit at Swimbridge, the screens at Kenton and Bridford, the celure at Hennock,

amongst others—but to my mind the finest example is at Dittisham. Though now but a pale shadow of its original splendour, it yet acts as a reminder of the richness of an English church interior of the fourteenth or fifteenth centuries.

There are about ten thousand mediæval churches in Britain, and the majority of these would have blazed with a polychromatic resplendence of which our cool, post-Puritan souls can have no imagining. Their columns, capitals and mouldings would have been painted. Their walls would have been covered with murals of saints, scriptural subjects and moralities. Their woodwork would have gleamed with colour and gilding. Their stained glass windows would have shone with something of the jewelled intensity of contemporary illuminations. Their floors (and particularly their chancel floors) would have been covered with patterned and encaustic tiles; there was a rich barbaric splendour about these places, expressive of their triumphant faith.

Much of this has disappeared; we live in the long winter of the Christian faith. Nonetheless, it remains impossible to find a mediæval church which does not contain at least one object of startling beauty—perhaps the head of an angel or a carved capital, a fragment of glass or the painting of a saint. It is a stimulating reflection that our Devonshire churches remain not only a palimpsest of many periods, the tangible expression of English history, but a melancholy reminder of our present lack of creative vitality.

Devon churches with remarkable pulpits include Dolton, Stoke Canon, Buckland in the Moor, Holne, Dartmouth (St. Saviour), Harberton, Swimbridge and Chittlehampton.

ST. MARY'S, ATHERINGTON

Unlike the churches of Torbryan, Ashton, King's Nympton or Harberton, St. Mary's in the village of Atherington near Barnstaple is far from spectacular: it is a quiet place, irregularly visited, a little fusty and often very cold. Yet, however muddled and minor its architecture may be, the church has served the people of its parish as a place of prayer and devotion, a place where the faith has been taught and the sacraments administered, for at least ten centuries. Its present fabric is the result of a constant process of evolution over centuries, each generation adapting and improving it in accordance with its ideas of what was fitting. The continuity of creation is very vivid here.

The first church was probably built between 1202 and 1272, but tangible records of its dedication have never been found. Nevertheless, St. Mary's is richly endowed (as most churches are) with a number of dateable artefacts: the recumbent effigy of a cross-legged knight (c.1240); the tomb of Sir Ralph Bassett and his wife Elinor (she died in 1349); a chancel screen (1425); some fragments of mediæval glass (1480); an octagonal fifteenth-century font and another Bassett tomb (c.1530). The latter rests in the so-called Bassett aisle, before which stands the church's most outstanding monument—its oak screen and rood loft (the only one in Devon), which add distinction to an interior which might otherwise be described as ordinary, if not dull.

Both are masterpieces of sixteenth-century carpentry, their carving rich with clotted stems, fruits and buds; the spandrels alive with little Italianate putti and Green men. The names of their "Carpenters, Carvers and Joiners" were John Parry of Northlew (who started it but for some reason then withdrew), and Roger Down and John Hyll of Chittlehampton, which lies but three miles distant from Atherington. Their work of flawless beauty was completed between 1544 and 1547.

After this there was both anticlimax and an emptiness: a long gap of almost two centuries when seemingly nothing happened, at least in the way of church embellishment. Then a flicker: in 1707, the family of the yeoman Anthony Snell erected a small but handsome tablet in his memory; a century later, in 1825 and 1863, the church saw the erection of further small memorials, many to members of the ubiquitous Chichester family. Meanwhile, in 1786, the lofty tower received a glorious Peel of six bells. One is inscribed 'Peace and Good Neighbourhood'.

But this was as nothing compared to the dislocation which disturbed and excited the village when Mrs Bassett of Watermouth Castle agreed to pay for the church's 'restoration' in 1882. The work, which included the partial rebuilding of the walls and the renewal of all

the windows, was supervised by John Loughborough Pearson (1817-97), the architect of Truro cathedral and St. Augustine's, Kilburn.

It was a late and last flowering, for, as far as the church's fabric is concerned, the story of the last hundred years has been a depressing one. In 1884, a Lychgate was added; thirteen years later an organ; and in 1953, a new altar and rereros—both, alas, unworthy to stand alongside the great sixteenth-century rood screen.

Devon churches with lavishly decorated screens include Ashton, Bovey Tracey, Bridford, Broadhempston, Colebrooke, Colyton, Dunchideock, Harberton, Kenn, Kenton, Ottery St. Mary, Swimbridge, Staverton, Torbryan and Totnes.

Rood screen tracery at St. Mary's, Atherington.

ST. MARY'S, HONEYCHURCH

Life is strewn with those miracles for which people who love beauty can always hope. One of these is a church near North Tawton—its name as delicious as its fabric.

It is very simple: an almost untouched twelfth-century building, to which a west tower and a south porch (which faces Dartmoor) were added in the late fifteenth century: in the tower are three mediæval bells in their original cage. Within the church's cream-washed walls there is a Norman font with a silvery wooden Jacobean cover, two twelfth-century corbels, an Elizabethan pulpit, a Victorian harmonium and, on occasion, a simple vase of flowers—and little else except clear daylight. Yet this humble interior is filled with a plenitude of life, everlasting goodness and harmony, which more famous and splendid churches do not always possess. It seems flooded in a lake of silence. Here the present is enough.

But the church of Honeychurch does not rest alone: it is surrounded by tombstones and a walnut tree, and beyond these, the parish of 607 acres, probably carved out of the north-western corner of the large parish of Sampford Courtenay when Huna built the first church in the tenth century. From the Domesday Book we can obtain a picture of the manor at that time; today its five farms, as depicted in 1086, remain practically unchanged. Then there was Walter's demesne farm, now Middleton, owned by the Reddaways. The four villein farms—Westacott, Slade, East Town and Hillside—are still being farmed; others include the Glebe and, further towards Exbourne, Bude.

The population of the parish has declined: 66 in 1801, 59 in 1851, 44 in 1901 and 21 people today; but in other respects, as Jose Reddaway tells me ("and I'm not telling any fibbers"), it remains largely the same. The hedgerows have barely altered, the farm entrances are the same, the fields are unchanged. In the church there is a monthly service which six parishioners regularly attend, and more at festivals. They care for the building: replace slates, cut the churchyard grass and contribute its heating oil. It has no electricity, and candles are lit on dark winter afternoons.

According to W.G. Hoskins, who wrote the leaflet about (and on sale in) the church, Walter's farm was worked at the time of Domesday Book by four slaves. I pointed this out to Jose Reddaway. "Oh yes," she retorted with the good humour which characterises those who live fulfilling lives, "it still is. And I'm one of them."

Other especially beautiful Devonshire churches include Ashton, King's Nympton, Molland, Parracombe, Torbryan, Hartland, Satterleigh and West Ogwell.

The simple interior of St. Mary's, Honeychurch, near North Tawton.

EXETER CATHEDRAL

*Part of the west front and the twelfth-century
Norman tower of Exeter Cathedral.*

The building is in no way conspicuous until one enters the spacious Cathedral Green with its wide lawns, limes and fringe of vernacular houses, shops, and a hotel: red brick, timber-framed, stuccoed, stone-faced buildings of many ages. Today, they are one of Exeter's greatest visual pleasures.

The see of Exeter was founded in 1050, when the ancient Bishopric of Crediton and Cornwall was transferred here. A Norman cathedral, on the site of the ancient Saxon church, was built following the Conquest. Of this, the two substantial towers of the present cathedral remain; they dominate the later building with tier after tier of blind arcading, tiny narrow windows below, larger windows at the top, a monumental assertion of the faith they proclaim. Between them rises the Gothic church with its flying buttresses, its large traceried windows and long row of pinnacles, all responsive to the changing light. The West front is superb: a long horizontal screen of statues—seated figures of kings, standing figures of saints and angels, all occupying elaborate canopied niches.

The exterior is impressive but the interior, largely built between 1275 and 1369, is superb. The nave is warm in atmosphere, exquisite in colour and with its arches, triforium and clerestory moving uninterruptedly towards the east end it appears as lithe, silvery and organic as a birch wood in early spring. Stand at its western end and marvel at the ordered serenity of its tiereron vaulting, enjoy the splendour of its roof bosses (amongst the finest in the country), and share in a fulfilment as deep as sight can hold. "All the way to Heaven is Heaven", said Saint Catherine of Siena, and it is here.

The vaulted nave of Exeter Cathedral, the longest unbroken stretch of Gothic vaulting the world.

DARTINGTON HALL

View of Dartington Hall, the largest and most important mediæval house in the west of England.

According to Nikolaus Pevsner, Dartington Hall, near Totnes, "vies with Haddon Hall and Wingfield Manor in Derbyshire as the most spectacular domestic survival of late mediæval England." It is certainly the most significant major example of mediæval domestic architecture in the west of England, a building of fresh nobility and charm.

Originally the possession of the Martin family, Dartington passed to the Crown in 1386, and in 1388 was granted by Richard II to his half brother, John Holand, created Earl of Huntingdon the same year and later Duke of Exeter, who married John of Gaunt's second daughter. A poignant reminder of these origins can be found in the central feature of the stone vault to the porch tower: a coloured boss, the emblem of

Richard II who died in 1400. It displays a chained hart on a heraldic rose. The original buildings, which consisted of not one but two courtyards, were built between 1390 and 1399, a few years before the construction of the naves of Winchester and Canterbury.

The surviving buildings are grouped around a huge grassed courtyard. The hall range on the south side (consisting of the porch tower, upper and lower residential blocks, a kitchen and great hall) is the work of John Holand. Flanking the courtyard's west side is a range of lodgings, one group of which still retains the external stone staircase which originally led to self-contained apartments on the first floor. Although almost every part of the building is of interest, Dartington's *pièce de resistance* is its majestic hall, built on the grandest scale and amongst the finest of its date in the whole of England. Of the original fabric, apart from the walls relatively little remains; the five-bay open timber roof dates from this century, but it is a triumph of sensitive restoration. It was designed in 1931 by William Weir, on lines similar to those chosen by the original (and anonymous) master carpenter in the late fourteenth century. In fact, since no drawings survived (and the original roof had been removed in 1813), Weir based his work on the outline of the mediæval roof timbers in the plaster at the west end of the hall.

To visit Dartington Hall, to wander amongst its soft dove-grey limestone walls, to listen to great music under the brown cats-cradle of its magisterial hall, to walk in springtime through its magnolia-scented paths, pause to admire its heavenly Buddha or catch the sight of swifts circling round its old church tower, is to discover for oneself an order of things loved and forever made beautiful.

The north-west corner of the Dartington courtyard, showing the stairs to an upper chamber.

THE DARTMOOR LONGHOUSE

A Devon longhouse: Bowden's Farm, near Ashburton.

Wherever our ancestors built with local materials, regional characteristics were unconsciously apparent: sandstone roofs in Sussex, slate roofs in Westmoreland, flint masonry in Suffolk and cob and thatch in Devonshire. The great houses of Saltram or Knighthayes might have been built anywhere in England, but the Devon cottage and the Devon farm building, especially the single-storey granite longhouse which is to be found only on and around Dartmoor, are literally built out of the local landscape. They belong to the earth and serve its purposes with grace and economy.

Although the Devon longhouse looks similar to the county's other farmhouses, it is fundamentally different: a dual-purpose building, providing human and animal shelter under a common roof. Our peasant forbears never withdrew from their cattle, but kept them under a single roof. To do so, they constructed a central cross passage to divide their own living quarters from the cow house, or shippon.

Although such a form of construction is well known on the continent, there are in modern England perhaps only about a hundred surviving examples, and less than twenty-five with the animal shelter unaltered; Dartmoor is the only area where they are to be found.

The average longhouse is one of the simplest and most economical forms of peasant house. Nonetheless, the form could also be adapted to show off the high social status of its owners. "Such longhouses," writes Peter Beacham, "are comparable in architectural sophistication and interior comforts and amenities not only with the best contemporary farmhouses anywhere in Devon but also any church or priest's house."

The Devon evidence suggests that the longhouse enjoyed a continuity of tradition from the early fifteenth to the late eighteenth century. Today, shippons are still used to shelter cows against the cold of a Dartmoor winter, or as stables, hen-houses, pigsties and lambing sheds; but such uses are a rarity.

One of the best surviving examples is Sanders at Lettaford, North Bovey. It is arranged on the usual plan of inner room, hall, cross passage and shippon, all under one roof, with a shouldered granite porch originally used as an entrance for both people and cattle.

The porch of a late mediæval longhouse: Sanders, Lettaford, North Bovey.

CADHAY

*An exquisite Tudor manor house: Cadhay, near
Ottery St. Mary, built between 1546 and 1550.*

Cadhay is a Tudor manor house a mile to the north-west of Ottery St. Mary. Modest in scale and ambition in relation to the so-called prodigy houses of Queen Elizabeth's reign—Longleat, Wollaton Hall, Hardwick Hall, Burghley House and Montacute—it is a singularly attractive building nonetheless. Most of its fabric is of Salcombe sandstone with dressings from the famous quarry of Beer which had earlier supplied stone for Exeter Cathedral.

The present building was built on the site of an earlier house, about which little is known. Between 1546 and 1550 it was extended, if not largely rebuilt, by John Haydon, a successful lawyer, bencher of Lincoln's Inn and legal advisor to the City of Exeter. Haydon had been appointed a Commissioner with responsibilities for winding up the monastic houses in this part of Devon, in particular the Scholastic Order in Ottery St. Mary, which took place in 1545. The King, by Royal Charter, also made four local gentlemen Governors of the Church of St. Mary, which had previously been under the control of the warden. Haydon was one of these. There is no evidence to suggest that he benefited financially, but in building his house at Cadhay he made free use of the stone from the demolished College buildings.

In this respect he was typical of the men whose houses were under construction at that time—houses like Little Leighs in Essex and Kirtling Hall in Cambridgeshire. Like Hayden, they too had managed to extract from the casualties of the time great advantage to themselves and, similarly, to show little artistic ambition. Like Cadhay, their houses were 'assembled'

rather than 'designed'.

The so-called Court of Sovereigns, Cadhay's most original feature, is especially attractive. It consists of a paved internal courtyard, entirely faced by checkerwork of sandstone and flint walls, a speciality of East Devon. In the centre of each side is a classical niche in which carved statues of Henry VIII, Edward VI, Mary and Elizabeth have been placed above the doors. These are the work of 1617, for that date appears under the niche which shelters the figure of Queen Elizabeth. Other attractive features include the east side of the house where mullioned casement windows remain, and the splendid curved timber roof chamber within the house.

Cadhay, the house and its grounds, is a perfect expression of the character of the English rural culture. More specifically, the house reveals the fundamental features of its Devonian manifestations. It is small in scale, unpretentious, and of an understated individuality.

Cadhay's internal courtyard: the Court of Sovereigns, c.1617.

LOUGHWOOD MEETING HOUSE

*Chaste perfection: Loughwood Meeting House,
Dalwood, near Axminster, c.1700.*

After the Elizabethan Settlement in 1563, the Anglican Church set about adapting its inherited buildings to fit the new liturgy and faith.

For the Nonconformists and Dissenters, there was no precedent. Feeling that the established Church had failed to throw off its ancient connection with Rome, they therefore set about the foundation of their own places of worship where, since the word was of primary importance, emphasis on preaching predominated. In Devon, a Baptist chapel is said to have been founded at Dartmouth as early as 1600, the next one at Plymouth in 1620, while others appeared at Kingsbridge and Kilmington in the following years. Altogether eight Baptist chapels appeared in Devon during the seventeenth century and seven more

were founded during the next hundred years. An example is Spicelands, near Culmstock, a meeting-house of the Society of Friends.

These chapels, and those of the Congregationalists, Unitarians, and later the Methodists, were usually no more than a room with practical fittings suited to their simple liturgical forms. Although unadorned, even austere, they can yet possess a quiet radiance and beauty of their own.

A typical example is the Loughwood Meeting House at Dalwood, four miles west of Axminster and virtually in the farmyard of Loughwood Farm. It was first mentioned in 1653 when a congregation in the village of Kilmington, some two miles to the south-east, sought refuge from persecution in a remoter place, the Lough Wood, then an area of dense woodland. The present Meeting House, dating from c.1700, still lies down a grassy track and amongst fields and trees; it is a simple, rubble-walled, thatched building with clear glass windows. Inside there is one large room furnished with a high-set pulpit approached by steps, unvarnished pine box pews and a gallery for the players of stringed instruments who accompanied the hymns—their music-rests are still in place, and in one position the book-rest has been cut away to accommodate the bass viol. Under boards there is also the all-important baptismal pool, whose water was obtained from a nearby spring. There is also stabling, a fireplace and a simple kitchen for the preparation of meals.

Loughwood Meeting House and burial ground once served as the rallying point of the East Devon Baptists, in the cruel days of persecution before the passing of the Acts of Indulgence (1687) and Toleration (1689) which permitted nonconformists to worship freely and openly.

Providence Methodist Chapel, near Throwleigh, built by the Bible Christians in 1839.

THE ADAM ROOMS AT SALTRAM

Of the great English architects, Inigo Jones, Christopher Wren, Nicholas Hawskmoor, John Vanbrugh, James Gibbs and William Chambers left no trace of their work in Devon. Yet their equals—Robert Taylor, Robert Adam, John Nash, William Butterfield, G.E. Street and Edward Lutyens—left buildings of considerable importance and distinction. These include Sir Robert Taylor's Palladian design for Sharpham House near Ashprington, John Nash's design for the castellated Luscombe Castle in Dawlish, Butterfield's and Street's two churches in Babbacombe (see page 82), Lutyens' baronial stronghold, Castle Drogo near Drewsteignton (see page 84), and Robert Adam's contribution to Saltram House near Plymouth. Of these, the latter is perhaps the most urbane and imposing.

The commission came in 1768 when John Parker (Lord Borington), a Member of Parliament, racehorse owner, farmer, countryman and friend of Sir Joshua Reynolds (who was born nearby at Plympton St. Maurice), asked the London-based architect, Robert Adam (1728-92) to bring his house up to date. Adam, an innovator who specialised in the design of country and London houses, obliged: his executed work for Saltram—the Saloon in 1770-72 and Dining Room in 1780-81—with their subtle colouring, elegant proportions and fastidious refinement of detail, remain to this day the showpieces of the house.

The huge Saloon, used for country balls, concerts and other entertainments, is one of his most splendid creations. To achieve an effect of total unity Adam designed all the fixtures and fittings down to the minutiae. The ceiling, boldly decorated with painted roundels within lozenges, is his; the echoing design for the Axminster carpet is his, as are the Venetian window, the neoclassical doorcases (with capitals derived from Diocletian's palace at Split), the gilded door handles, the four great looking-glasses, the overmantle, the gilded torchères and, in all probability, the pair of monumental side-tables. The gilded suite of eighteen armchairs and two sofas (upholstered in the most delicate ice-blue damask) have been attributed to Thomas Chippendale. The overmantle has also affinities with a Chippendale drawing for a frame at Nostell Priory, suggesting that he may have been responsible for the design; but even if this were so, from first to last the Saloon is an Adam room.

The Dining Room (originally fitted up as a Library) has something of the same exquisite refinement. With a cool green and stone colour scheme, its carpet also echoes the circular pattern of the ceiling. No less thematically integrated, exquisite and delicately restrained, are the room's basket grate, fender and irons, vases and pedestals.

There can be no doubt that Adam's work for Saltram helped to create feelings of aristocratic and luxurious pleasure for those who frequented it (the Saloon is said to have cost at least £10,000), but the symbolic richness and imaginative virility that had characterised England's mediæval architecture was by that time a thing of the past. Saltram may be the most impressive country house in Devon but it is not, alas, a house of soul. It cannot inflame the heart or uplift the spirit. The numinous lies beyond the power of its elegance; beyond the age of secular achievement; beyond the eighteenth century as a whole.

The Saloon at Saltram House near Plymouth, designed by Robert Adam between 1768 and 1781.

ALL SAINTS, BABBACOMBE

The Victorians began a great period of English church building, which at least in quantity is comparable with the fifteenth century. In the 1840s more churches were built in Devon than in any other decade of its entire history. At least thirty-two were either under construction or being wholly rebuilt, many by John Hayward, Devon's most prolific nineteenth-century designer. Such churches were being erected not only in the towns, but in such isolated places as Twitchen on Exmoor, East Woolfardisworthy, Bere Alston and Alfington—the last by William Butterfield (1814-1900). In the Three Towns—Plymouth, Devonport and Stonehouse—nine new parishes were formed in seven years under Sir Robert Peel's New Parishes Act.

Church-building continued on a large scale in the 1860s; important additions included Butterfield's All Saints in Babbacombe, and Street's St. John's (1861, but tower 1884), also in Torquay. In fact no less than ten new churches were constructed in that town between 1846 and 1896. Butterfield, a major Victorian architect, also designed and built churches at Yealmpton (1850) as well as restoring existing ones in Ottery St. Mary and Abbotskerswell.

There are, I admit, many who find his architecture wilful and discordant, but I am not one of them. I love his moral feeling and the intensity of his religious passion.

The tower and spire of All Saints, Babbacombe, designed by William Butterfield between 1865 and 1874.

For me his work not only represents the spirit of his age—the confidence and the fear of the first industrial nation at the height of its power, but at its best—as at All Saints, Babbacombe (1865-7, east end and tower 1872-4)—a song of triumph.

The interior is concealed by a grey stone exterior but its nave reveals an extraordinary, even ferocious confidence. The basic shapes and masses are boldly simple but the surfaces are sumptuously rich. Pevsner found the surface treatment "both fascinating and repellent" and the poet Gerard Manley Hopkins felt "its oddness at first outweighed its beauty". In fact the church's interior is a magnificent assertion of sensuous delight as its use of colour alone expresses: marble columns of dark veined browns, outer walls of reddish sandstone, upper walls of red and dark grey patterned in grey and buff; font and pulpit of rich yellow, black, dusty pink and gleaming white; and in the chancel floor a wonderful composition of pinks, grey-blues and buffs, with highlights of black, sea-green and veined yellow. Butterfield delighted to use every coloured stone, marble and other material he could find for the money at his disposal. But he was a severely practical man, and a planner and constructor first. His decoration was meant to emphasise his construction.

Butterfield built for the glory of God. All Saints may be accused of hardness and severity but these, like its honesty, were born of his faith. In that, as in so much else, he followed in the path of his mediæval predecessors.

The interior of All Saints, Babbacombe, as it appeared in the Edwardian period.

CASTLE DROGO

On the end of a great rocky promontory overlooking panoramic views of the river Teign, stands a spectacular house, Castle Drogo. Completed in 1930, it is perhaps the last country mansion of its kind, certainly the last castle to be built in England, and one of its architect's most famous and extraordinary masterpieces.

It was built for Julius Drewe, who had conceived the idea of a castle to satisfy his dream of becoming a country gentleman living in a baronial stronghold. It was therefore unsurprising that Drewe chose the architect to whom the successful middle classes were turning for large or small houses in the country, to realise his unusual brief. Sir Edwin Lutyens (1869-1944), the greatest British architect of the twentieth century, was

Castle Drogo, near Drewsteignton. Designed by Sir Edwin Lutyens, it was the last castle to be built in England.

a prodigious worker, his output totalling about 400 projects including the two greatest commissions of the age: the layout for the new capital for the British Raj and the Roman Catholic Cathedral in Liverpool.

The original brief included a vast courtyard entered by a gatehouse but with the plan going through several changes over a ten-year period, only a fraction of this was eventually built. The result is a building about a third of the size originally intended. Nonetheless, the completed fragment, as Pevsner says, "has a compelling but abrupt sublimity".

The interior is a different matter. On the whole the furnishings are mediocre and some of the rooms—the Dining and the Drawing Rooms, for example—are not entirely convincing. Nonetheless, the building's functional areas (including the main and service corridors, the staircases and suite of rooms composing the Kitchen, Scullery and Larder) are a triumph. They contain unexpected spatial effects, coffered granite vaults, shallow domes and pendentives as well as a superb use of materials which it is worth travelling half a day to enjoy. Here is Lutyens at his most stately, eloquent and unostentatiously monumental.

But if the complex planning of the staircase, which provides a monumental approach to the dining room and the vaulted main corridor, are very fine, the areas I value most are the 'below stairs' kitchen spaces. Here the

staff of living-in servants—butler, under-butler, cook, scullery maids, head housemaid, under-housemaid, two lady's maids, nanny and nursery maid—ministered to its wealthier occupants. For the former, Lutyens created a roof-lit Kitchen (with a round beechwood table and dresser to his design), a Larder with slate shelves and granite walls built around an octagonal well, besides a top-lit Scullery worthy of the serious art of food preparation: it possesses two monolithic columns, oak dish-racks, fitted tables and an hexagonal chopping board almost as monumental as the front porch. Castle Drogo cost a great deal of money—well over the original estimate of £60,000—and was 'finished' in 1930. But by that time not only had the Drewe's eldest son been killed at Ypres, but the First World War had forever marked the demise of the country house and the society of which it was the most potent symbol. By that time another radical break with the past had also taken place. In 1927, the architect Le Corbusier published his highly influential *Towards a New Architecture*, in which he articulated a vision of the future, a future in which architecture would owe no debt to tradition, to any form of picturesque variety, decorative complexity or use of local materials. By reducing design to a sterile minimalism that was truly cosmopolitan, it reflected neither place nor local culture, only an ideology of freedom through denial of the vernacular.

The Scullery at Castle Drogo.

THE DREAM CHURCH OF MILBER

St. Luke's, Milber, Newton Abbot. Begun in 1936, its plan was revealed in a dream.

The 1930s was not a decade which saw much, if any, distinguished architecture in Devon; at Dartington there is High Cross House (by the Swiss architect William Lescaze), but for all its merits it has as much to do with the county as a lion in Paignton Zoo. No less inauthentic was the housing then being built over the rural outskirts of Plymouth, Exeter and Barnstaple, with row upon row of characterless streets. Interestingly, it was in one of these estates about half a mile south-east of Newton Abbot that perhaps the county's most remarkable 'thirties building is to be found. It is the church of St. Luke's in Milber, based on a dream by a Devon man, the Rev J. Keble Martin (better known for his *British Flora*), whose brother Arthur designed it on the basis of the former's description and sketch plan.

Like many ideas discredited by rationalism, the dream has had a long and powerful influence on the history of the human race. From the shamans of Malaysia and North America, to the traditions of the biblical, Koranic and Hindu religions, it has provided knowledge about precognition, healing and ecstatic insight. But rarely, if ever, has it been the source of a church design—at least in this century. On 11th March 1931 Keble Martin experienced an "odd and vivid" dream in which he attended a crowded evening service at a church which did not then exist. The following morning he made a note of its unusual design: no screen dividing clergy from the congregation but in its place an open sanctuary in immediate contact with the body of worshippers; no Gothic nave but in its place three radiating 'transepts'. He then showed the design to his brother,

who produced a somewhat conventionalised interpretation: a St. Andrew's cross imposed on a long nave with an apsed chancel—the design that was later built.

A start was made with the Lady Chapel in 1936, but the church was only completed in 1963. It is, I must say, the most extraordinary building. There is something of the Byzantine about it and something modern; it is dreamlike, and yet, with its Cornish granite rough-hewn columns, earthy. The interior is flooded with natural light and painted a luminous white; its apsidal sanctuary, curved ceiling and harmonious arches create a feeling of almost heavenly ethereality. A strange feature of the design is that when its plans were completed it was found that its proportions, without being intentionally so, were exactly a thousand inches long, a thousand inches wide and a thousand inches high.

It did not take long for someone to recall the line about the Temple in Revelations: "The length and the breadth and the height of it are equal."

The Oratory of Holy Baptism, St. Luke's Church.

CHAPTER FOUR:

Images & Objects

Give me to fashion a thing;
Give me to shape and to mould;
I have found out the song I can sing,
I am happy, delivered and bold.

Laurence Binyon, c.1920

Some of the seventeen children of Sir Amyas Bamfylde and his wife,
Elizabeth Clifton, in All Saints, North Molton. Dated 1626.

A PREHISTORIC WOODEN FIGURE

The earliest accurately dated evidence of human existence to be found in Devon (and indeed, in Europe) was discovered in 1927, when a team of people digging near the entrance of Kent's Cavern in Torquay uncovered a jawbone with three teeth. Subsequent radiocarbon investigation has dated it at 31,000 years old.

Another significant object to be discovered in Devon is the prehistoric wooden figure (illustrated on the next page) unearthed by workmen digging ball clay at Zitherixon, Kingsteignton, in 1867. According to one nineteenth-century account, the figure was discovered "in a standing position 23 feet below the surface against a black oak tree which was embedded in mud, sand and gravel and lying on the deposit of large stones."

The figure, which is 34 cm. tall and carved from the centre of an oak branch, was probably fashioned (according to radiocarbon dating carried out by Oxford University) between 426 and 352 B.C. Although there is no recognised certainty as to its original purpose, it may be related to the tree worship of a period when it was still believed that trees had a spirit to be venerated with prayers, offerings and circumambulations. In modern India there are still thousands of sacred trees, whose special sanctity is enhanced by rituals. To fell one is a sacrilege and quite unpardonable. A not dissimilar sense of veneration for the spirit world is to be discovered in contemporary Japan, where I have seen both trees and rocks sometimes bound by heavy plaited ropes (*shimenawa*). In the religion of Shinto, the sun, water, trees, rock formations and even sounds are sometimes worshipped because it is believed that they are inhabited by gods (*kami*).

The Celts certainly endowed features of their environment—a river, spring, tree, mountain or simply a particular valley or habitat—with a similar sanctity; many topographical names still demonstrate the close link between divinity and the land. For these, too, the gods were everywhere; everything possessed holiness.

Little is known about the objects used in Celtic liturgy apart from the ritual vessel or cauldron, but sacred idols, images and votive offerings undoubtedly played a part in their ceremonies, as they do in India to this day. Most of the objects which have survived are of stone, but some wooden examples fashioned of oak heart-wood have been discovered. The very large number that have survived is indicative of the great quantities which must have been in existence at one time or another. The Roman author Lucan (39-65), describing a Celtic forest-sanctuary at Massilia (near Marseille) that was violated and destroyed by Caesar, explicitly refers to such sculptures:

"And there were many dark springs running there, and grim-faced figures of gods uncouthly hewn by the axe from the untrimmed tree-trunks, rotted to whiteness."

Yet pagan images celebrating the old gods and spirits of nature did not die out with the Celts, the Romans or the Dark Ages. The perennial symbol of our unity with nature, the Green Man, is a figure to be found in many Devon churches. Amongst these are Sampford Courtenay, South Tawton, Spreyton, Ugborough, North Bovey and High Bickington, which has thirty-seven examples. There are also some sixty-six Green Men in Exeter Cathedral alone. North Devon possesses an exceptional number of Green Man carvings of the fourteenth and fifteenth centuries, such as those at King's Nympton, whose pub, interestingly enough, is still called The Grove.

Many other villages bear the word Nymet, Nymph or Nympton in their names: all derive from the Celtic word *nemeton*. Nymet meant a sanctuary or consecrated place, and probably indicates that there was a pagan sacred woodland grove in which was set up an altar.

A wooden figure, dating from c.426-352 B.C. On loan to Exeter City Musems.

A ROMAN BRONZE FIGURE

The sea-abraded bronze reproduced on the opposite page represents the young Achilles equipped with bow and quiver, riding on his tutor Cheiron, who has the figure of a Centaur: the body of a horse, and the trunk and head of a man. Cheiron has raised his left hand to his face, as if searching for a distant quarry; but as he does so a wild beast, probably a dog, leaps at one of his forelegs.

John Allan writes that the group comes from the top of an elaborate Roman folding tripod. "Such furnishings had three uprights, each topped with a group of figures, connected to each other by diagonal bars. Flat trays, bowls or basins could be held within." A tripod of this kind must have adorned a villa or temple, although none has been discovered.

The bronze, which is 18 cm. high, was found by fishermen on Sidmouth beach close to the mouth of the river Sid in 1840. It was recognised as a Roman artifact by the local antiquaries Peter Orlando Hutchinson and N.S. Heineken, and in 1871 was presented to Exeter Museum by the Rev. Heineken.

The Roman occupation of this island, which marks a turning point in the country's emergence from prehistory to history (and lasted a full half-millennium) begins in 55 and 54 B.C. when Julius Caesar launched his two expeditions into Britain. They brought him nowhere near Dumnonia (the Roman name for modern Cornwall, Devon and that part of Somerset west of the river Parrett), but following the invasion in A.D. 47, the Claudian armies occupied Britain as far as the Severn and the Trent. By A.D. 55, their legions were in the most westerly of their towns, Exeter, called *Isca*. Here, the second Legion built a fort of thirty-six acres and fortified it with a palisade and bank. Later they were to extend this site into a full Roman city contained within the bounds of the present city walls and establishing the template of all its major streets. From Exeter a road was built towards North Tawton where a marching camp and a Roman station were established. There were also forts at Okehampton, a settlement (possibly a port) at Topsham and evidence of military activity elsewhere.

Although Roman Exeter was a sophisticated city, and the area we now call Devon was dotted with fine villas and large estates, the impact of Roman civilisation on the inhabitants of the region was probably small. Apart from coinage, there is extraordinarily little surviving evidence from the three centuries of Roman rule, which ended in A.D. 410 when the legions left Britain and the native rulers took their place. It was in these later years that the bronze figure was presumably lost; it has been dated to about the second century A.D.

Bronze figure of Cheiron, with Achilles on his back; second century A.D.
The original is in the collection of Exeter City Museums.

MEDIÆVAL IRONWORK

Detail of ironwork on a door in St. Saviour's, Dartmouth.

The traditions of the blacksmith in Britain are of undoubted antiquity; certainly the craft existed a long time before the Roman invasion. Yet little survives of the work of those early years apart from the hinges and strapwork on certain church doors. Some of these show a considerable ornamental elaboration, with arabesques like those from the backgrounds of illuminated miniatures. A much later example is to be found on the door of the church of St. Saviour in Dartmouth.

Originally the south door, the ironwork boldly bears the date 1631, but in all probability it dates from the late fourteenth or fifteenth century and was repaired, as a note suggests, at the later date. Functional, but beautiful and dignified, the work depicts the Tree of Life guarded by beasts—the two Lions of Edward I, who died in 1307. These form the strap hinges stretching across the width of the door.

Dartmouth is rich in exceptional artefacts. In St. Saviour's there is an unusually complete rood screen and a stone pulpit with a frieze of enormous leaves. In St. Clement's there is a Norman font and a handsome piscina. St. Petrox, close to the castle, is superbly sited. The town is also endowed with handsome buildings of many periods, including the four timber-framed houses built between 1628 and 1640 known as the Butterwalk, which is Dartmouth's pride. I love best the door of St. Saviour's.

It is so assured, so unostentatious, so poetic; its leaves reminiscent of the Devon landscape, all its flowers and trees in full growth; its rampant lions suggestive of the lost England of the imagination; its Tree of Life, linking earth and heaven, rooted in darkness, its crown expanding into the light. The vitality of that ironwork, so quintessentially Devonian in its spirit, is also a reminder, as the historian of the period, John Harvey, suggests, of the unquenchable confidence of the people of the Gothic age. "The Gothic men," he writes, "were certain of themselves, knew where they wanted to go and went, well assured that their paths led to God. In their eagerness to build, and to build magnificently; in their love of exuberant ornament and profusion of every form of art; in their underlying hatred of usury and sharp practice and their belief in the just price; above all in their love of gaiety and bright colour, of song and dance, of ceremonial and humour everywhere, even in church, the men and women of the Gothic age proved themselves truly human, and more than human. The final refutation of the materialist, the rationalist, the sceptic, lies in the tangible, unsurpassable remains of Gothic art."

The door of St. Saviour's.

BEATUS & BOSSES

As stated, Exeter's cathedral is as a building unparalleled in Devonshire; none other approaches it in beauty or thrilling imaginative power. But its wonderfully rich interior is not a bare nave; it is also embellished with stone screens, sedilia, stained glass, furnishings of every date, and a lavish array of over a thousand carvings including a collection of 370 coloured roof bosses, second in quality only to those at Norwich.

It is known that these date from the last quarter of the thirteenth century at the east end to the second half of the fourteenth century in the nave. And because more mediæval fabric rolls are still in existence at Exeter than anywhere else in Britain, it has been possible to identify some of the carvers by name: William of Montacute and perhaps two others.

The bosses depict a variety of subjects: some figural, others purely decorative; some employing traditional religious symbolism, others unashamedly secular in their interest. There are heads, including eight heads of kings and five heads of queens; several full-length religious

scenes including the Coronation of the Virgin and an angel playing a harp. There is also a boss of an eagle carrying off a pig, others of dogs chasing rabbits and squirrels eating nuts, as well as a mermaid holding a fish. In addition, there are many Green Men inside the cathedral: they start in the Lady Chapel, constructed in the earliest part to be built in the rebuilding programme which began in 1275 and continued over the next eighty years.

No one seems to have found a key to any unitary iconographic sequence in the programme of these works, which seem to have been arranged in a rather haphazard way: sacred images being juxtaposed with profane; elevated devotional themes with images drawn from sources outside the learned traditions of the church. But the comprehensive, even encyclopædic vision of these bosses is especially attractive: the whole world is here: the freakish and the saintly, the cosmic and the popular; pigs, goats, birds and dragons and, in

A boss of Christ in Majesty: the central figure is flanked by winged angels bearing ritual flabella, *or fans. It dates from 1353.*

the crucifixion, the story of God's redemption of humankind.

Inevitably, the quality varies. There are some with naturalistic foliage, others with a courtly charm, yet others with a leaning towards the decorative; but without exception each is carved with an organic and natural quality evoking a feeling of forceful energy and primordial life. And if, on occasion, there is bloodshed and pain—in for, example, the boss depicting the murder of St. Thomas at Canterbury—the prevailing mood is one of praise and happiness—an attitude summed up in the epitaph of Hugues de Doignies, a lay brother and goldsmith in a monastery near Namur in about 1300:

Ore canunt alii Christum: canit arte fabrili Hugo
Let others sing Christ with their mouths: Hugues
    sings with his goldsmith's work.

A lovely example of this underlying joyfulness is the coloured boss illustrated on the previous page. It is an image of Christ in Majesty, probably copied from an early mediæval manuscript in which kings are commonly depicted in this fashion.

A further source of inspiration for the bosses were the bestiaries, the mediæval books of beasts. The example on this page is taken from another source: an early thirteenth century Psalter, originally used in the church of St. Helen's, Worcester, before it reached Exeter in or about 1275. In this beautiful illumination several monsters 'inhabit' great coils of knotted, interlacing tendrils. The physique of the mediæval dragon, although not firmly fixed, usually included a bulbous body, wings, two feet with lion or bird claws, and a long curling tail.

Of course, the delineation of this beast was far from literal but what freedom it allowed the distant regions of the human mind! What scope for the imagination unshackled by 'realism' and scientific accuracy! What poetic fancy grew from it—as indeed it does here.

The initial B from the Beatus page (beginning of Psalm I) of a thirteenth-century Psalter now in the Exeter Cathedral Library.

HARVEST JUGS

This jug, from the collection of Exeter City Museums, is a heart-moving example of the work produced in North Devon throughout the seventeenth and eighteenth centuries. On its globular lead-glazed body, as ripe and golden as a fruit, there is a drawing of a huntsman and his hounds pursuing a rabbit. The vessel, dated 1703, also has a long inscription in verse.

Domestic pottery was being made in the Barnstaple and Bideford area from the thirteenth to the early twentieth centuries. Potters were working in Bideford in mediæval times, but the first to be described as such was a Thomas Chope, who could have been working in the town since 1596. Like other local potters, Chope made use of the red- or chocolate-coloured Fremington clay for the body of the ware and the white ball clay from Peters Marland near Hatherleigh for slip and mixing glazes. At the beginning of the seventeenth century, due mainly to one puritan family, the manufacture of pottery was the most important industry in Bideford. In 1672, twenty-one men were at work with six master potters in the town.

The industry thrived over such a long period principally because large quantities of red clay were available in the locality, and the nearby estuaries of the rivers Taw and Torridge enabled profitable expansion of sea trade. In fact North Devon wares were exported to

A North Devon harvest jug, belonging to Exeter City Museums.

Wales, Ireland, Northern Europe and the New World. Home markets also flourished as communities demanded a wide range of useful wares for many aspects of domestic and social life—butter-pots, shallow bowls, pitchers, crocks, baking pans and the like. The more elaborate were sometimes decorated with designs being cut through a coat of slip to reveal the different clay underneath—the so-called *sgraffito* technique (after the Italian 'to scratch'). In addition to their everyday, functional use, Harvest Jugs (made between 1698—the year of the first example, which is now in America—and the end of the nineteenth century), were made primarily as decorative objects; many as gifts or to commemorate specific events such as marriages, betrothals, anniversaries and, of course, the successful harvest. The wide variety of subjects illustrated on their sides includes ships, lions, unicorns, birds, flowers, and harvest and hunting scenes.

North Devon pottery can be seen in the North Devon Maritime Museum in Appledore, the Museum of Barnstaple and North Devon in Barnstaple, the Burton Art Gallery and Museum in Bideford and the Royal Albert Memorial Museum in Exeter. The Victoria and Albert Museum in London, the Swansea Museum and the Fitzwilliam Museum in Cambridge also possess examples.

A North Devon harvest jug, made by John Hollamore on June 4th, 1748. It is one of two magnificent examples in the collection of Swansea Museum.

DEVON CLOCKS

Before the correlation between use and beauty was ended—a division which took place at the Industrial Revolution—the beauty of an artifact was in variably a by-product of its fitness for the purpose for which it was made. The vaulted nave of Exeter cathedral was essential to its structure; the ironwork of St. Saviour's door was dictated by its function; the design of a farm-cart was imposed by usage—a usage closely related to, as the wheelwright and author George Sturt has explained, "the nature of the soil in this or that farm, the gradient of this or that hill, the temper of this or that customer or his choice perhaps in horseflesh." Thus the necessary requirement of any design was that it should fulfil its purpose, whether primarily material (as in the case of a wagon or a door), or primarily spiritual, as with a church, but often some mixture of the two.

Nonetheless, if the primary reason for the manufacture of an object was utilitarian, its utility was inseparable from its beauty. Consider any Celtic artifact; enter any Gothic cathedral, any village church built before the mid-eighteenth century, any early manor house, any English market town; regard any seventeenth-century printed book or drinking glass, any eighteenth-century silverware, and you are left with a tingling sense of pleasure at the rightness of their craftsmanship.

Amongst the thousands of such craftsmen are the clockmakers whose work, touched by luxuriances of beauty, is sometimes so dazzling that it can summon up a whole culture.

A typical clock-making and watch-making establishment in a Devon city or town at the end of the eighteenth century would have consisted of the master, his family, a journeyman, and possibly two or three living-in apprentices. Although watch repairs were invariably carried out on a bench by the front window of the shop, anyone making up the clocks usually worked out of sight in a workshop at the back of the premises. In his study of Devon clocks and clockmakers, Clive N. Ponsford writes that "in the larger city retail businesses it was not unusual for a jeweller to sell ready-made clocks and watches, or to employ working watchmakers and silversmiths, and vice versa; and the names of jewellers, goldsmiths and silversmiths will be found on watches and the dials of clocks." Covering the period from the fourteenth century to about 1900, he lists the names of 1,750 clock- and watch-

Brass Lantern Pendulum Clock by Abell Cottey of Crediton, c.1680. It belongs to the Exeter City Museums.

makers who lived and worked in Devonshire, their craft being practised in virtually every town.

The tradition of fine work established by 'William Clement Totness' was continued there by William Stumbels, a craftsman of superb capacity who had previously worked at Aveton Gifford near Kingsbridge. Stumbels specialised in chiming longcase and other clocks for the owners of some of the county's principal country houses. Among his patrons were the, Champernowne, Carew, Ibert and Courtenay families. A fine example is still to be seen in the latter's castle, Powderham; this is the so-called Equation Clock, for which he was paid one hundred guineas. Its complex dial is perhaps the finest the master made. The layout is masterly and the finish luxuriant. In his book *Devonshire Clockmakers*, J.K. Bellchambers claims that William Stumbels was probably the most brilliant clockmaker of his time outside London.

The architect Christopher Wren caused to be inscribed on his tomb in St. Paul's the words *Si monumentum requiris, circumspice* (If you seek my monument, look around you). May we not say the same of England's many craftsmen?

Dial of the so-called Equation Clock made by William Stumbels for the Courtenay family between 1743 and 1747. It is in Powderham Castle.

HONITON LACE

Cosimo de Medici visited the West Country in 1669 and reported that "there is not a cottage in all the county [of Devon] nor that of Somerset, where white lace is not made in great quantities so that not only the whole kingdom is supplied with it but it is exported in great abundance."

The lace industry he viewed is said to have been introduced into Devon in the early sixteenth century, but it may have been in existence before that date. Thomas Westcote mentions it around 1630 as though it were not a new trade. Of Honiton, he writes: "Here is made abundance of bone lace, a pretty toy now greatly in request," and he further mentions that it was made at Bradninch also.

By the end of the seventeenth century the industry had spread into all the East Devon parishes, where it was often made by lacemakers in their homes. By 1699 there were over 4,700 people employed, the largest centres being Honiton and Ottery St. Mary. Colyton, Beer, Seaton, Sidbury and Sidmouth had more than 300 workers each. The trade continued to flourish throughout the eighteenth century until the time of the French Revolution, which brought about a change of fashion. Thereafter muslins and gauzes became the rage.

At the beginning of the nineteenth century, the decline was aggravated by the introduction of

machine-made net, which threw hundreds of lace-workers out of work. As early as 1822 Lysons in *Magna Britannia* commented that of 2,400 lace-makers in Devon before 1816, only 300 remained. In the same year, John Heathcoat, a lace manufacturer of Loughborough in Leicestershire, who had been driven out of the Midlands by the Luddites, set up his machine-made net and lace factory in Tiverton—it employed 1,500 workers.

The slump in hand-made lace continued and was only temporarily abated by Queen Victoria's request that her wedding dress be made of Honiton lace at Beer and Branscombe. By 1887 the industry's depressed state

A detail from 'The Lacemaker' by Charles Stuart, dated 1885.

was sufficient to engage the attention of a parliamentary committee. At Beer, where there had been 400 lace-workers a generation earlier, now only sixty or seventy remained. At Exmouth, where twenty lace-schools had flourished, none was left in 1887.

But this reduction in the numbers of people employed and the loss of quality of their work was not unique to either hand-made lace or to Devonshire. In Bedfordshire, reed-matting and basket making, hemp-spinning and pillow-lace; in Buckingham, straw-plaiting; in Lincolnshire, linen-making; in Suffolk, wool-spinning and hempen cloth; in Essex, baisies and rope; in Hampshire, coarse woollens, bed-ticking and worsted yarn; in Kent, silk, parchment, leather and snuff; and in Oxfordshire, velvets, gloves and blankets—all were profoundly affected or even destroyed by the introduction of machine-based processes of manufacture. By 1851, only fifteen per cent of rural industries had survived the debacle; by 1930, only one per cent.

A century ago, the village of Finchingfield in Essex had two carpenters, two blacksmiths, a wheelwright, a plumber, a painter, a cooper, a glazier, a clocksmith, together with thatchers, millers and experts with the mill-bill for dressing the stones. At an earlier period, the list would have been more than double, with websters, weavers, cordwainers, tanners and turners as well. Today, Finchingfield would be fortunate to possess so much as a thatcher, and the same is true of Devon, where the dissolution of the whole structure of the old rural society has been no less complete.

A nineteenth-century example of Honiton lace by Mrs. C.E. Tradwin.

BLAKE AT ARLINGTON

'The Sea of Time and Place' by William Blake, dated 1821,
at Arlington Court near Barnstaple.

Although Devon has produced a number of famous visual artists, these have generally been of less repute than the major writers associated with, or born in, the county: Richard Hooker, Robert Herrick, Samuel Taylor Coleridge, Charles Kingsley, R.D. Blackmore and Henry Williamson. Nonetheless, Devon-born painters include the great miniaturist Nicholas Hilliard (1547-1619), born in Exeter, and the portraitist Sir Joshua Reynolds (1723-1792), born in Plympton. There are also the water-colourists Francis Towne (1739-1816) and John White Abbott (1763-1851), as well as numerous lesser talents: Thomas Hudson, James Northcote, Benjamin Robert Haydon, Charles Eastlake and Samuel Prout. The outstanding Devonshire artist to have been born this century—in Plymouth—was Cecil Collins (1908-1989).

In some ways Collins is the natural link with William Blake (1757-1827); both were deeply spiritual, metaphysical artists; both were neglected in their lifetimes; both prophets and visionaries as well as painters. But although one of Blake's most beautiful and important watercolours is at Arlington Court, north of Barnstaple, he never set foot in the West Country. In fact the painting, to my mind the most beautiful in the county, came to be in Devon almost by accident. When the National Trust took over Arlington Court in 1947, the picture was discovered still in its original gilt frame with its convex Vauxhall glass intact and signed 'W. Blake. Inventor, dated 1821.' How it came to be on one of the pantry cupboards is not known.

No less mysterious is the picture's subject, alternatively called *The Sea of Time and Space* or *The Circle of Life* or *The Arlington Court Picture*. The most specific identification so far, though not universally accepted, is that it shows the incident of the 'Cave of the Nymphs' from the Odyssey, perhaps by way of the Neo-Platonist interpretation by Porphyry. If that is so, the kneeling figure in red would be Odysseus, the pointing figure next to him Athena, and in the sea is Leucothea, the marine goddess, grasping a cloudy wreath above her head. This is the sea-girdle she lent to Odysseus, which enabled him to arrive home in safety; he has thrown it back to her as she is driven away by her sea-horses.

Athena points to the scene in the sky: Helios the sun-god asleep in his chariot surrounded by celestial nymphs. At the right is a stairway to the cave, from which flow water and fire; on the stairway, nymphs holding shuttles weave on a loom. The poet and Blake scholar Kathleen Raine claims that the subject is a representation of the cycle of life, symbolised by the traveller leaving his native shore and later returning; or the cycle from eternity, through life, to eternity.

Yet whatever its subject, this picture is one of most exultant of Blake's late works. Its range of brilliant visionary hues, its almost Botticellian grace, its freshness, fluidity and overall radiance make it amongst the loveliest of this artist's works.

"The Man who never in his Mind & Thoughts travel'd to Heaven is No Artist," he wrote. And here, amongst the cabinets of bijou bric-à-brac—glass elephants, model ships and decorated porcelain—in the Ante Room of Arlington Court, is a vision as paradisical as anyone can hope to find in earthy Devon.

THE STAVERTON PARISH MAP

A pictorial map of the village of Staverton, near Totnes, made by its parishioners between 1993 and 1996.

I also asked (the Squire of Norton) if he had never tried to establish, or advocated, or suggested to them any kind of reunion to take place from time to time, or an entertainment or festival to get them to come pleasantly together, making a brightness in their lives—something which would not be cricket or football, nor any form of sport for a few of the men, all the others being mere lookers-on and the women and children left out altogether; something which would be for and include everyone, from the oldest grey labourer no longer able to work to the toddling little ones; something of their own invention, peculiar to Norton, which would be their pride and make their village dearer to them?

From *A Foot in England* by W.H. Hudson (1909)

There are owls, a dragonfly and a chaffinch, a red fox and a kingfisher, two churches, a grand mansion, a view of the river, a famous mediæval bridge and, yes, a red car, a pylon and a tractor; it is an image of the 600-person parish of Staverton at the end of the twentieth century. It is a map celebrating the life, the buildings, the countryside, the birds and beasts of this extensive parish in the green, curvaceous countryside of the South Hams. According to Susan Misselbrook, who co-ordinated the project (and who works as a visual artist at Paignton Zoo), the map involved the skills and creative energies of just over a hundred parishioners and took three years—from the autumn of 1993 to December 1996—to complete. Those who participated included children from Landscove Primary School, who created the border of flora and fauna; a young carpet-layer in his early thirties, who embroidered the steepled church; members of Staverton Women's Institute, who quilted all the pieces; as well as men and women aged over seventy. According to my rough count, the map contains something under two hundred and fifty different segments, each of which has its own story.

To start the process moving, Susan Misselbrook called a public meeting, which produced the core of those who were to guide the map-making; some of these were primarily interested in the history of the parish; some, on the other hand, were more interested in the map's creation. It was the latter who decided that it should be the size of a double-bed sheet (86 inches by 100 inches) and made with a variety of fabric techniques: batik, wax-resist silk-screen and dyes. But whatever their interests, skills or length of residence in the parish, both groups had one and only one objective: the discovery and re-creation of all that delighted them in their own locality. "We live in a very pretty parish," Susan told those attending the initial meeting, "we are fortunate to be here. The map is our opportunity to display our love for this place. It is our opportunity to explore it, to express what we value here, our skills, our artistry, our creativity."

Making it, she tells me, was a marvellous community effort; "It may have been a bit sticky to begin with but after eighteen months things began to catch fire. People became inspired; their memories of Staverton, their regard for its distinctive features, lots of local history, what had happened in the past, their passions about the small and commonplace, all began to come out."

CHAPTER FIVE:

Traditions

*How, then, shall we define the valuable tradition? It is one with
a green end, or one that conceivably might, if attended to,
and for all its moribund appearance, venture a leaf.*

Laurence Whistler, 1947

*A loaf of bread, candle and book-rest on the altar of St. Peter's,
Dowland, near Hatherleigh. Harvest Festival, 1997.*

CHURCH BELLS IN DEVON

For fifteen hundred years the Christian religion has used bells to announce a service. When the first missionaries to these islands walked across the fields they rang small handbells to summon the people. No Saxon or Norman bells survive, but bells of the thirteenth, fourteenth and fifteenth centuries still hang in a few churches in every county, Devonshire included. The earliest bell left to us, dated 1296 (thousands were destroyed at the Reformation) is at Claughton in Lancashire. But at Cabersfield in Oxfordshire there is a bell, presented by Hugh Gargate, the Lord of the Manor, who is known to have died in 1219. Devon has more bells than any other English county—about 2,800. Like Cornwall, it also has its own distinct style of ringing, called 'call-change' ringing. This is the method whereby instead of changing the order of the bells in the ring, the pattern changes under the direction of a leader. For this reason the standard of striking in Devonshire is exceptionally high, and in this county there are more ringing competitions than anywhere else in Britain.

I have this information from the Reverend Prebendary John Scott, whom I have known for thirty years. John, who has made a life-time study of bells and climbed nearly all of Devon's 300 church towers, has been Diocesan Advisor on bells for the last thirty-five years. For a certainty he knows more about the subject

of Devon bells than anyone else now living. "When people have problems with them," he tells me, "I scratch around among the jackdaws' nests and tell them what needs doing." With his white beard and noble build, John Scott could be mistaken for an old-time sea captain, but it is bells, their history, their ringing, their naming, their casting and their technicalities which have captured his

West window and bell-ringers' ropes in
St. James', King's Nympton, near Chulmleigh.

imagination since, at Oxford, he learnt to ring. "It is music, heavy engineering—and people," he explains with characteristic vigour. "The nice thing about the English ring—one man per bell—is that it is also a team activity, a social occupation. It is a part of the social fabric of a community. At Down St. Mary and South Tawton, for instance, you find very keen ringing places."

"Tiverton, Chulmleigh, Tavistock, Totnes, Modbury, have exceptional bells. North Molton, with a beautiful ring of six, is also very fine, while the cathedral has the second heaviest bells in the world hung for ringing full circle." Many of these, he says, were cast in the eighteenth century, when Devonians took up the art of ringing in earnest: from the 1730s onwards, they also began to increase the number of bells employed—from three to as many as six or eight. Devon's oldest bells date from before 1340. "As far as I know there is one of this age at Haccombe, two at Bulkworthy and another two at Petton, near Bampton, which was once part of my parish. The oldest to be run full circle is at Peters Marland, which was cast by a man who is known to have been working in the early 1300s. It has the handsomest lettering in Latin."

I asked John Scott why people rang bells, what their pleasure was in ringing them. There were, he said, many different motives, including the joy of coordinated team-work, delight in the creation of a beautiful sound and the intellectual satisfaction to be found in the sustenance of a complex pattern. In addition, there was the excitement of being able to control something bigger than you are with some degree of refinement. "Even though a ringer may be controlling a bell that weighs up

to two tons, the difference between a well struck and a not-so-well struck blow is in a hundredth of a second." "Bells are there for the glory of God but I can say on the basis of a lifetime's experience that people ring them for all kinds of reasons as well as that one."

A new tenor bell being added to the five existing mid-eighteenth-century ones at St. Edmund's, Dolton. The date is 1921.

DECORATING THE PARISH CHURCH

Lilies scent and decorate the church.

Robert Stephen Hawker (1804-75), the Cornish poet and antiquary, was curate of Welcombe, near Hartland in North Devon, for thirty years; he held the living with that of Morwenstow, where he lived and with which he will be forever associated. There Hawker repaired the well of St. Morwenna, kept ten cats and introduced the Arthurian cycle to Tennyson. It is also to him that we owe the Thanksgiving Service or Harvest Festival.

In the summer of 1843 he issued a notice to his congregation, inviting them to receive the sacrament on the following Sunday "in the bread of the new corn". Thus, building on the ancient Lammas festival, when the first sheaf of the harvest is cut, he created a new one: the Harvest Festival. Writing thirty years later, his biographer, Sabine Baring-Gould (see page 149) observed that "there is scarcely a church in England in which a Harvest Thanksgiving Service is not held." This is true to this day. With its air of offered gratitude, earth-loving generosity and eminently singable hymns, it continues to remain one of the best loved and attended in the English sacred year.

Harvest Thanksgiving is generally at evensong. But the church is decorated throughout the day with pools of glistening apples, potatoes and turnips, loaves of bread, great dropsical marrows, bunches of mauve Michaelmas daisies and golden sheaves of wheat.

But autumn is not the only season when churches are embellished. At Easter the women of the parish bring in great sprays of budding leaves—cherry blossom and horse chestnut—armfuls of bewitching daffodils, primroses from the hedgerows and forsythia from gardens. On window sills, around pulpits and in front of mediæval screens, they will place further sprays. In a corner of the church they may also have prepared a tray of bright green mosses and selected stones to act as a reminder of Golgotha or the Sepulchre. It, too, will be dewy, scented, verdant, like the greater resurrection of the world outside the church.

For hundreds of years Devon churches have been decorated in ways that express and appeal to the senses and the soul. The employment of flowers is a common practice. Their use may not be one that is specifically Devonian but nonetheless it is one that flourishes in the county today; almost every porch contains a rota; almost every church at least one vase or bowl of flowers. It is a practice that relates nature to religion and both to art.

Autumn flowers decorate the reading desk in
St. Peter's, Dowland. Harvest Festival 1997.

DEVON CIDER

The word cider derives from the Latin *sicers*, meaning a strong drink. It is a beverage especially associated with Devon, where its manufacture is of some antiquity. Hoskins reports that on the Earl of Devon's manor of Exminster the bailiff's account for the year 1285-6 shows cider-making on a considerable scale.

Centuries later, Hooker, in his unprinted *Synopsis Chorographical* of about 1600, refers to the great abundance of fruit of all kinds in Devon, and to the careful management of the orchards and apple gardens. One

Detail of 'The Cyder Feast', a wood engraving by Devon-born Edward Calvert, 1828.

reason for this is that in Elizabethan times, cider was sold in large quantities for the provisioning of ships. It was also a tradition to pay part of a farm worker's wages in cider. In the nineteenth century, a typical allowance would be from three to four pints a day, increased to six to eight pints in August, during harvest.

Until the 1950s, orchards were widespread throughout the British Isles. Almost every farm had its orchard and made its own cider. But in the last half century the total orchard area under cultivation has declined by about two thirds—around 150,000 acres have been lost. Almost 90% of Devon's orchards have been grubbed up in recent years.

I met Norman Hancock, a 66-year-old cider maker, to learn at first hand something of this ancient craft. He owns and works at Clapworthy Mill, in a beautiful flat-bottomed valley near South Molton. For five generations, for over 100 years, the Hancock family have been making cider in the same vicinity: Norman's great-grandfather at Middle Blackpool; his grandfather at New Barn at King's Nympton; his father first at King's Satterleigh and latterly at Clapworthy, which he purchased in 1957. The apples from Norman's twelve-acre orchard are supplemented by others from as far away as Exbridge and Crediton, which include Crimson Kings, Russets and Newton Wonders—note the loveliness of both the old apple and village names. Others include Yarlington

Mill, Chisel Jersey, Brown Snouts, Velbrie and the famous Devon varieties, Pigs Nose and Slack-me-Girdle.

On a fresh spring morning, Norman Hancock showed me around the site. In the dark interior of the main shed, filled with presses, barrels and retorts, he explained the different stages of cider manufacture: how the apples are first milled or crushed, how the juice is then extracted from the pulp (or pummace) by pressure in a so-called 'cheese', how it is then fermented (which takes anything from one to four years) and then bottled in 2 and 2 1/2 litre casks. From 100 tons of fruit, about 15,000 gallons of cider are produced every year.

Yet although the sun was shining, the setting idyllic and the drink delicious, all is far from well at Clapworthy. The duty on cider, business rates, the pressure of work, competition from the larger manufacturers (sadly, most pubs prefer guaranteed year-long sameness: "Our cider varies because of the different apples," he said) are presenting problems to which he returned again and again. How to continue to exist? His daughter works for the business, but for pay significantly less than she could earn elsewhere; his wife assists with the tourists, upon whose purchases Hancock's Devon Cider depends for its survival. But his son is absent: he has become a computer programmer. I asked Norman Hancock if he liked his own product. "Oh, yes!" he replied, "but there is simply too much to do."

Norman Hancock at Clapworthy Mill.

THE VILLAGE PUB

The Duke of York, Iddesleigh.

The origins of the English pub probably lie in the Roman *tabernae vinariae*, shops where wine and food were served to customers seated on stools around a communal table. Yet in spite of this, the oldest English pubs only date back to about the eleventh century; one of these, The Church House at Rattery near Totnes, is in Devon. England has few alehouses of this antiquity, but as places of hospitality and refreshment for travellers, from Elizabethan times onwards the inn, alehouse, public house or tavern started to become much commoner. After the introduction of the first Turnpike Act of 1663 and the establishment of a better road system, the coaching inn became even more ubiquitous.

But the English country inn was never the resort of wayfarers alone, for in all ages the ale-bench has been the social centre of the town, village and hamlet.

Devon has no shortage of exceptional pubs. These include The Nobody Inn at Doddiscombsleigh, The Drewe Arms at Broadhembury, The Olde Globe at Berrynarbor and The Cott at Dartington, but my favourite is probably The Duke of York at Iddesleigh, near Hatherleigh. The present inn not only stands in one of Devon's most beautiful and unspoilt villages but faces south towards the blue line of the Dartmoor hills.

The present owner, Jamie Stewart, has traced back the names of nineteen licensees to 1850, when an Aaron Manning ran the pub. But in my mind it is Sean and Peggie Rafferty, its licensees from 1945 to 1974, who will be forever associated with The Duke of York.

It is an extraordinary inn and has it seems attracted another extraordinary licensee. Although born in Sussex, Jamie Stewart once lived and went to school in this little known area north of Dartmoor—reason enough, he believes, for his and his wife's return. Fifteen years ago they purchased a house in Winkleigh, and in 1996 achieved their ambition to own and run The Duke of York. Yet running a country inn is, he tells me, no easy task. "It's only recently that country pubs have made a living. The licensees once used to supplement their income: the wife ran the bar, the husband farmed some land. And if this county still possesses the largest number of free houses in Britain, it is sad to report that Devon has been losing its pubs on a regular basis since the last war. Nonetheless, I don't doubt that it's possible to run a rural inn and to do so quite well financially. It's a long-term enterprise and I intend to succeed."

Jamie Stewart exudes the qualities essential to the success that he has already achieved: some ninety per cent of the inn's customers continue to come from within a radius of ten miles, and the dining room is invariably oversubscribed. Yet an achievement of this kind does not come without hard work and a professionalism of which he is understandably proud. With residents, the day can start at 7.30 and end at midnight—or beyond. I left in the knowledge that The Duke was in good hands.

The Elephant's Nest at Horndon, near Mary Tavy, north of Tavistock.

DEVONSHIRE DIALECT

A gathering of farm workers at Peagham Barton,
near St. Giles in the Wood, Torrington.

The Shorter Oxford English Dictionary defines dialect as "a variety of language arising from local peculiarities" or "a variety of speech differing from the standard language, a provincial method of speech".

To my mind, dialect is also a form of spoken language that enriches and gives character to the modern tongue. This is not, I accept, the view of those whose aim is to iron out all that deviates from the accepted, standardised norm, be it B.B.C. English, Mass Media English, Public School English, Oxford English, and the like. Yet one has only to contrast the latter's dessicated and abstracted nature, invariably coagulated with fashionable urban slang, with the speech of those who still speak the old language, full of good concrete imagery, to know what is being lost.

I know the truth of this from two sources: on the one hand, the ever-more trivial forms of communication which are heard in public places and, on the other, the conversations I enjoyed with our neighbours, an old gamekeeper and his wife, in the North Yorkshire village where we once lived. The speech rhythms, diction and vocabulary of these two were virile and substantial, wonderfully alive, and with the kind of musicality to be found in Chaucer. When they spoke, their language was informed by a feeling for the flow and flux of life; it belonged to the world that they so intimately knew: the world of earth and weather, animals and farming; the world of people who addressed each other directly, face to face. In contrast, the bloodless and impersonal language of the average modern town-dweller seems to belong to the world of computers, consumerism and the media.

Coming to Devonshire in the sixties, I was astonished and delighted to hear the burr on the tongue. Today, that burr is less apparent; decades of 'education', of television and advertising, have done their straightening job. Yet Cecil Torr, with a delicious sense of comedy yoked to a fastidious exactitude, reminds us in the following passage what the richness of the Devonshire dialect was once like.

It comes from Part I of *Small Talk at Wreyland*, which was published in 1918:

Devonshire speech is not capricious, but has a syntax of its own. The classic phrase is 'her told she'. A pious person told me that 'us didn't love He. 'twas Him loved we.' They never say 'we are,' but 'us be' or else 'we am,' contracted into 'we'm.' They say 'I be' as well as 'I'm' but never 'me'm' or 'me be,' though invariably 'me and Jarge be', or 'me and Urn,' or whatever the name is, and never 'Ernest and I' or 'George and I.' They say 'to' for 'at'—'her liveth to Moreton'—and formerly said 'at' for 'to'—'I'd be going' at Bovey'—but now it is the fashion to say 'as far as' Bovey. A complete Grammar might be compiled.

Happily the school has not taught them English that is truly up to date. They have not learned to say: "The weather conditions being favourable, the psychological moment was indulged in.' They still say:- "As 'twere fine, us did'n'." And their pronunciation is unchanged: beetles are bittles, beans are banes, and Torquay is Tarkay.

COB & THATCH

Although the thatched cottage has become irrefutably associated with Devonshire, thatch and cob (or reed, straw, heather or some similar vegetable product and different combinations of locally available unbaked earths) have been employed for centuries, as have other local materials. In Gujarat, on the Ivory Coast, in Senegal and the Amazonian rainforests, cob and thatch have been used since the distant past. Such materials are easy to find and practical to live in; an igloo of perfect security. They are vernacular, unpretentious, economical and beautiful. Yet the owner of one of South Devon's prim pink colour-washed cob and thatch cottages (clematis and carriage lamps round the door) is now enjoying the former home of a peasant who had not the least pretension about his house.

Mud is just wet earth. To be suitable for building, it must contain sufficient lime to enable it to set, and usually it needs to be mixed with chopped straw, and for preference also ballast (gravel or other small stones) and sand. Cob is essentially the same: it is on-site subsoil mixed with straw, sand, other aggregates and sometimes dung. The widely varying nature of the subsoils in the county have an inevitable effect on the techniques of mixing and building. As a material, so long as it is kept dry, cob is enduring; it can last for centuries. Devon, in fact, has examples dating from the sixteenth and many from the seventeenth centuries. Cob is an exquisite natural material, sympathetic to the local terrain and character.

Cob and thatch at Gittisham, near Honiton.

Yet if the use of cob is now in abeyance, the craft of thatching is flourishing. The use of thatch (if the term be stretched to embrace the roughest brushwood), was formerly widespread, as in many parts of the world it remains to this day. There are references to thatch by the Venerable Bede, who died in 735, and it was almost certainly employed before his time. After 1200, although thatch was already beginning to fall out of general use for the roofing of buildings of importance, it continued to be the commonest form of roof in most parts of the country until well into the Tudor period. Thereafter, reflecting the geographical distribution of such materials as slate and stone, the use of thatch became more localised; the widespread use of cob in Devonshire from the fifteenth to the nineteenth centuries (and the county possesses more 'unbaked earth' buildings than any other in Britain), largely accounts for the extensive use of thatch.

Aesthetically, this was a happy circumstance, for an undulating, smooth reed roof surmounting walls of creamy unbaked earths creates an effect at once homely, comfortable and domesticated. It is coherent with much of Devon's gentle countryside and unmistakably, enrichingly, it contributes to its special character. For what moves me so much about the traditional cob and thatch cottage is the harmony of buildings made out of and blending into the surrounding landscape. Simple, functional, as they are they yet give expression to a way of life, an order in utility, that gives serenity to the interior and beauty to the exterior.

See page 165 for the story of a young Devon thatcher, James Marshall.

Thatched cottages at Broadhembury (top), Winkleigh (middle), and Coleford (bottom).

THE CIRCLING YEAR

Fire festival at Torrington, November 1974.

The cycle of the year—winter followed by spring, then summer and autumn—has been imprinted on the life of Earth for billions of years. Little surprise, then, that our ancestors responded so fully to the circling year. For them there was no mistaking the days of darkness, mistletoe and ice and the midwinter splash of light. The new time of spring: the universal cycle of death, renewal, fulfilment and waning were all marked. At a later time, the Christian calendar sustained the universal cycle of life—Christmas and the winter solstice, Easter and spring—with many observances, feasts, play cycles, ceremonies, parish and calendar days, all serving to articulate instincts and energies which were never exclusively Christian.

Before the turn of the century, Devon people were involved in a complex series of calendar events, some Christian, some not. Some are still preserved, some not. Some were celebrated in all communities, some in only one. Many of these were attached to particular seasons and events in the agricultural years: to Midwinter and Midsummer, to the spring and autumn equinoxes, to ploughing and sowing, the springing of the corn and harvesting. Amongst the commonest I would include: Wassailing (5th January), Plough Monday (first Monday after Twelfth Night), Shrove-tide and Ash Wednesday (the beginning of Lent), Mothering Sunday (fourth Sunday in Lent), Lady Day (25th March and, of course, a Quarter Day), Maundy Thursday (the day before Good Friday), Good Friday, April Fool's Day (1st April), St. George's Day (23rd April), Mark's Eve (24th April), May Day and Garland Day (both 1st May), Oak Apple Day (29th May), Lammas (1st August), Michaelmas (29th September), Halloween (end of October), Guy Fawkes Day (5th November); also the Ashen faggot, and the Christmas Mumming Plays known to have been performed at Exeter, Tiverton, Stoke Gabriel, Broad Clyst, Ashburton, Dartington, Silverton, Bovey Tracey and Sidmouth.

Today, the ritual element is no longer part of life. The traditions with which the calendar was once celebrated have been watered down or even lost, yet there remains a rich tradition of festivals and events. In my own area of North Devon, the following are celebrated on an annual basis: Torrington's May Fair, where the town centre is decorated with branches of flowering gorse; the procession in memory of the martyrdom of St. Urith (or Hieritha) in Chittlehampton on 8th July; Chulmleigh Old Fair, during which a white glove, garlanded with red roses, is ceremoniously thrust through a window of the Town Hall on the last Tuesday in July; the Fire Festival in Hatherleigh, when at dawn on 5th November a sledge of tar-barrels is set alight and run down the hill that leads through the town.

On the same day, the turning of the Devil's Boulder, in the village of Shebbear, is also celebrated. Another annual event is Combe Martin's The Hunting of the Earl of Rone. Its celebration was said to mark the anniversary of the capture of an Irish refugee, the Earl of Tyrone, who landed nearby and lived for a time in woods near the village, existing on sailors' biscuits, which he wore as a necklace. If the story is correct, the custom would date from the reign of Elizabeth I, when a rebellion in Ireland was led by the Earl of Tyrone; but certain elements in the pageant, including the Fool, the Hobby-Horse and the attempts to cure the fallen Earl, would seem, by analogy with similar practices in other parts of the country, to be much older.

DEVONSHIRE CLOTTED CREAM

Eleven types of cream are produced in Britain, ranging from pasteurised single cream to the richest of them all, farmhouse clotted cream. Devonshire clotted cream is of the greatest antiquity; we know this because the dairies on the Tavistock Abbey estates in the early fourteenth century had no churns for butter-making, but raised the famous clotted cream by scalding the milk. The cream, when cold, was then stirred, and butter produced in that way. The Cistercian monks of Tavistock and their tenants were undoubtedly familiar with clotted cream as a result of this process. Indeed, the method of making it is so elementary that it may date as far back as the domestication of the cow.

In my early twenties I first learned how cream was made. I was then living on a farm in the village of Colyford near Seaton where, in return for my keep, I acted at weekends and on holidays as a relief milker. The farmer's wife, Mrs Pady, regularly made a bowl of delicious clotted cream from the high butterfat milk of her beloved Jersey cows. Each and every day she placed their milk in the cool of the farmhouse dairy and left it for at least six hours, a process she called 'settling'. This was followed by the scalding, wherein the bowl of milk, now placed in a larger bowl of cold water, was left overnight on the slow fire of her kitchen range. Next morning, the pan was cooled for another six hours

before its layer of golden cream was skimmed off the milk base. At Dare's Farm it was eaten with just about everything except vegetables and meat.

The old spellings, "clowtyd, clouted, clowted, clawted, clotted", are descriptive of the thick, folded, yellow, granular substance Mrs Pady made for pleasure and for sale. In those days in the early fifties she ran her own 'pin-money' business sending cream by post in quarter- and half-pound round metal containers.

More recently, I visited Hawkridge Farm (or Barton) in Umberleigh to learn about another method; in this case demonstrated by Valerie Hosking and her husband, John. Their cream is made in a Diabolo Cream Separator from the untreated milk of their herd of 40 Friesians.

From a postcard inscribed "Real Devonshire Cream - a Dartmoor Farm scalding the milk." Date and place unknown.

Some time back, as her mother had done before her, Valerie Hosking made it twice a week, but now makes it only for special occasions.

The Diabolo is a heavy-duty machine, turned by hand; about five gallons of milk will produce about two pounds of cream in ten to fifteen minutes. In their cool, capacious larder, it was bolted to a thick slate shelf: Valerie Hosking showed me how it was put together; her husband turned the handle until there was a high pitched whirr, and cream and butter fat spurted out of different spouts. Just as they say you can tell the sounds of the 'working' of the cider if you listen with your ear to the cask, so you can tell, he told me, when the cream was ready.

John Hosking has lived and worked at Hawkridge all his life, as did his father. The farm nestles in a hidden valley, its thatched roof echoing the hillside's slopes; its stone was quarried locally, and its timbers originally hewn from local trees. Although the house dates back to the fourteenth century (traces of the original thatch have been discovered under later layers), it was not until 1560, when the second son of John Acland married Agnes, daughter of Courtney of Molland, that the Aclands took up residence in Hawkridge Barton. In 1615, the house was reconditioned and a plaster overmantle fashioned over the fireplace in the main room. The work depicts the story of Adam and Eve in the garden of Eden. In that quiet Eden we nibbled biscuits and drank tea. Valerie Hosking told me that before this book has been published, she and her husband will have retired to a bungalow in the next village. She expressed her fear that

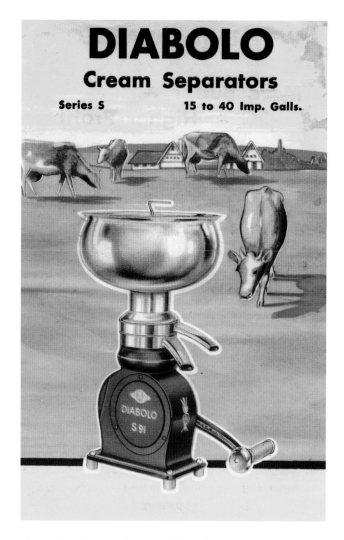

thereafter Hawkridge would no longer be a farm. Pig slaughter, cider-making and bread-making had already ceased. Cream would go next.

1930s instruction manual for the Diabolo Cream Separator, formerly in use at Hawkridge Farm, Umberleigh.

SONG AND DANCE

The folk collector Cecil Sharp once described England as "a nest of singing birds". At the seasonal feasts and practices, at the Whitsun-ales, at the festivals of the plough, at weddings, wakes, harvest suppers, and the great central event in the pastoral calendar, May Day, singing (and dancing) were commonplace for centuries. Singing of this kind, often communal but sometimes solitary, was no idle whimsy, a vanity to pass the time between one day and another. It was an attempt to come to terms with certain mysterious matters in a people's surroundings and circumstances. To explain and console, to eradicate drudgery, to provide entertainment and, on occasion, give expression to some of the profoundest aspects of human life, including sexuality—such was the purpose of traditional song. Thus for centuries it was one of the mainstays of our culture, of our life.

The singing continued long into the nineteenth century, until the decline of cottage industries and agriculture

Broadside woodcut of the song 'Death and the Lady', from the archive of Sabine Baring-Gould preserved at Killerton House, near Exeter.

so impoverished rural life that both singing and the tradition of seasonal festivities came to an end. "The girls who sang at their milking and the women who sang in their kitchens now preferred," writes James Reeves, "hymns to ballads. The young men regarded the modal music of their fathers as behind the times and preferred the productions of the music hall. Evangelical religion frowned upon the wantonness and license of the songs which, as a boy, Baring-Gould had heard in the parlours of Dartmoor taverns." In such circumstances it became a matter of urgency to save the unwritten inheritance of the people before it perished with the old singers.

For Devon, the most important of the folk song collectors was Sabine (pronounced Sabian) Baring-Gould (see page 149). In 1887, when he was over fifty, he turned his full attention to this formidable task. From 1888 to 1890 he contacted over sixty old men and several women singers, many unnamed; these included Robert Hard, a former road-mender from South Brent, and James Parson, an old hedger who lived in Lewdown and was nicknamed 'the Singing Machine' because of his remarkable memory and seemingly inexhaustible repertoire. "He was very strict with me," wrote Baring-Gould, "and insisted on my taking down his airs correctly. "Thicky wi'nt do," he would say, "you've gotten that note not right. You mun know that I'm the master and you'm the scholar."

Sabine Baring-Gould is now recognised as the chief saviour of West Country and specifically Devonian folk-songs, of which he collected at least 700. One hundred and ten of these were published in a single volume in 1892 as *Songs and Ballads of the West: A Collection made from the Mouths of the People.* Although his handling of the material is often questioned, without his efforts it is probable that the bulk of Devon's traditional songs would have been lost forever. *Strawberry Fair* and *Widecombe Fair*, the latter probably a relic of a lost folk custom, are two of those he rescued from potential oblivion.

According to Mick Bramich, an authority on Baring-Gould and a Totnes-based teacher of music and children with special needs, the singing that enriched the towns and villages of the past has never fully died out. "I even suspect," he told me, "that there are more young people involved in traditional music than at any other time in the twentieth century. Now they are singing in the back bars of pubs, and alongside them, but in an entirely different category, are the travellers—the dog and horse dealers who gather at events like the Bampton Horse Fair and Tavistock Goosey Fair. Step dancing is another tradition carried forward by the travellers."

A society that lives by manufacture and commerce is apt to forget its roots in the activities of the past; the traditional music and dance of previous centuries becomes of almost no concern. It is therefore good to learn that there are those who continue to draw inspiration, solace and joy from such a natural form of self-expression.

Folk dancing at Kingford Hall, High Bickington.
Date unknown, but probably 1920s.

CHAPTER SIX:

Occupations

Man should be prouder of having invented the hammer and nail than of having created masterpieces of imitation.

Hegel

Trawlers in Brixham harbour, 1997.

FARMING

Although by far the greater part of Devon's population is now urban—600,000 out of a total population of 1,049,000 people live in Plymouth, Torbay and Exeter—Devon remains a predominantly agricultural county. It also has a highly cultivated landscape, the product of more than fifty generations of farmers tilling or grazing the land.

Most of the county's farms are of the greatest antiquity; about two-thirds existed before 1066. Farming expanded throughout the twelfth, thirteenth and fourteenth centuries. At the time of the Black Death (1348), the high water mark of mediæval farming had been reached, but thereafter it was only to face decline, after  the plague eliminated about half the population.

The great rural prosperity of the sixteenth and seventeenth centuries is borne out not only by a study of contemporary tax assessments but by the evidence of the substantial rebuilding of Devon farmsteads, many of which date from the years 1560-1640. By the seventeenth century, the county's farming was so good that it elicited the praise of no less than Oliver Cromwell,

himself a landowner.

Yet if at the time of the Stuarts the Devonshire farmer was enjoying a measured prosperity, within two hundred years farming standards were falling, and falling fast. The endless cycle of its up and downs continued and have never been better demonstrated than during the last two hundred years. The war years of 1793-1815 brought prosperity; the coming of peace, its opposite. Decline was also exacerbated by the introduction of cheap American and Canadian corn which in the late 1870s and 1880s brought about a calamitous fall in prices. By the year 1938 arable land under cultivation was down by a quarter of a million acres from its 1872 peak. But even this figure hides the full impact of the industrialisation of farming which began in the nineteenth century.

Farm workers and their families, then living under conditions more wretched than at any time since the Middle Ages, had already began to migrate to better paid work in the towns. Village populations reached their peak about 1850 but between then and 1901 some

Dornafield Farmyard, near Ipplepen, South Devon, with horned South Devon cattle and shire horses. 1922.

371,000 folk (more or less the total population of Devon at the beginning of the nineteenth century) left the county to find work elsewhere. The population of most inland villages was halved. Today, in Devonshire, apart from farmers and their wives, less than ten thousand people are employed in agriculture, hunting and forestry.

These figures describe a catastrophe that is now virtually complete—though many farmers argue that it is getting worse. Yet there must surely be a limit to this destruction and Hoskins, in his *History from the Farm*, tells us why. "Men must eat and drink before all else: and the food-grower—the farmer—is the foundation of human society. You do not destroy the farmer unless you wish to destroy the whole of society."

Sheep being rounded up at Densham Farm,
near Ashreigney, North Devon, in 1981.

131

MINING & EXTRACTION

The mineral resources of Devon are exceptionally rich. Yet although small-scale mining for tin, iron, lead, silver, gold, arsenic, wolfram and copper have been carried out for centuries in its many parishes, there have been only two large-scale instances of mineral extraction in the county's history. The first of these took place in the Tamar valley, where rich deposits of copper and arsenic were discovered in 1884 at Blanchdown, overlooking the

Miners at Spreacombe Iron Works, Georgeham, 1872.

The richest copper mine in Europe had been discovered.

In quick succession, as the lode was followed eastwards, other mines came into being, their titles reading (as Frank Booker, the historian of the Industrial Archæology of the Tamar Valley, remarks) like a handlist of Victorian Christian names. The last, Wheal Emma, was named after Mrs William Morris, mother of the poet, whose husband (and his brothers) had purchased 314 of the original 1,024 £1 shares. Ironically, the apostle of handicraft relied on their income (£819 in 1857; £780 in 1859) to subsidise his work until he disposed of them in 1875.

Tamar above Gunnislake. It was then that the Duke of Bedford leased some ground to a group known as the Devonshire Great Consolidated Copper Mining Company, a name later shortened to the Devon Great Consols. In November of that year prospectors struck a rich copper lode; this marked the beginning of an enterprise that was to galvanise Tavistock and the entire area, explode the port of Morwellham into prosperity, treble the local population, employ at its peak over 1,200 people (including nearly 400 children), produce more than £4,000,000 worth of minerals, 736,000 tons of copper, 72,000 tons of arsenic—and pay £1,225,216 in dividends.

Yet by that date the quays were deserted, the mines closed. The unrestricted flowering on an exploitative economy was represented by the despoliation of some eight acres of once beautiful land: by massive unemployment, by no less massive spoil heaps, by broken flutes, by ruined buildings, by empty cuttings and, at Morwellham, by an empty dock basin gradually filling with mud and silt.

The other major enterprise, the extraction of china clay, no less environmentally dramatic, has already been discussed (see page 42).

(see page 42).

The earliest known photograph of Morwellham, c.1870.

THE CLOTH INDUSTRY

The importance of sheep to the economy of Devon, and the extent of the county's cloth trade in the sixteenth and seventeenth centuries, can hardly be exaggerated. Almost all the wool that Devon needed for cloth-making came from its own sheep; thousands of shearmen, combers, weavers, spinners, dyers and other workers were employed in its processing. At one time virtually every Devon village would have had spinners and weavers working away in their cottages to supply the cloth merchants in the towns.

Cloth-making for home use was practised in the county from earliest times. Records show that both wool

A great wool church: the Lane aisle in
St. Andrew's, Cullompton, c.1526.

and cloth were being exported from the South-West by the thirteenth century. Exeter was the earliest centre; there are also signs of manufacture at Totnes before 1200. Elsewhere in Devon, the rising cloth industry was to become responsible for the development of towns such as South Molton, Honiton, Ashburton, Tiverton and Culmstock. Most of the county's small towns, and quite a few of her larger villages—Landkey for example—also seem to have been centres of cloth manufacture at least up to the time of the Black Death, which decimated the population. Some idea of the scale of the industry at this time can be gathered from the fact that whereas the whole of Cornwall sold but 205 cloths, Devon merchants sold 8,235—an annual sale of over 100,000 yards of cloth.

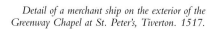

In the early fifteenth century Tiverton was an insignificant market town, largely dependent on the Courtenay household in the castle. By 1600 it had become the largest and most flourishing industrial community in the county. The town's most successful cloth merchants were John Greenway (who beautified its parish church with a chantry chapel completed in 1517 and decorated it with a frieze of merchant ships) and Peter Blundell (who founded its famous school in 1599). Both started life with nothing, and built up extensive fortunes in the Tiverton cloth trade. And at another east Devon cloth centre, Cullompton, my namesake, John Lane (d.1529), also glorified his local church with the addition of a fan-vaulted aisle, built between 1526-9 on its south side.

Soon after 1600, the Devonshire woollen industry, which had risen to wealth on the production of light fabrics of worsted-type cloth (known as kerseys), moved over to the production of serges or perpetuanos: fine, hard-wearing, long-lasting cloths, as their name indicates. The 'new draperies' as they were called, made Exeter extremely prosperous. With the Restoration, the Devonshire cloth industry expanded vigorously, turning increasingly to the manufacture of serges for the Dutch, German, and Spanish markets. For a period of around thirty years up to 1715, the Devonshire serge industry was the most important branch of the great English woollen industry, at least in the field of exports. But the continental wars of the eighteenth century gradually killed the overseas markets for serges.

Later in the century, the rise of Yorkshire woollens knocked out both the East Anglian and Devonshire cloth industries. The latter's trade, already dwindling, had by the middle of the century received its death blow from the Napoleonic wars. In 1838 there were still thirty-nine spinning mills in the county, employing more than three thousand looms in weaving serges. But towards the end of the century, the mills fell out one by one. In 1881 there were only about 1,200 people in the whole county employed in the woollen and worsted manufactures. Today there is not one.

Detail of a merchant ship on the exterior of the Greenway Chapel at St. Peter's, Tiverton. 1517.

FISHING

A turn-of-the-century photograph of fishing boats at Appledore.

With coastlines on the Bristol and English Channels, good harbours and flooded river valleys, Devon has played a notable role in the maritime history of England, at least until the 1820s. With a tradition of seamanship going back at least as far as 1550, Devonian enterprise was second to none. Fishing, exploration, commerce, privateering, smuggling and enterprises of war have been extensively carried on from her ports, while the high romanticism of Drake, Raleigh, Hawkins and Grenville will be forever associated with Devon.

By the 1560s, Devon's deep-sea fishing industry had already spread across the Atlantic to the rich cod fisheries of the Newfoundland Banks. This trade was to persist right through the next four centuries, ending only in 1930 with the sale of the last British sailing vessel, a schooner from Salcombe. But by the 1930s, fishing, the third most important of the county's historic industries—the others being textiles, and mining and quarrying—employed as few as only one Devonian in four hundred.

Although fishing has taken place from many creeks, beaches and small havens, notably Clovelly, Beer and Sidmouth, large-scale fishing enterprise has been historically associated with the county's southern coast. In the sixteenth century, Kingswear, Salcombe, Exmouth, Budleigh Salterton, Otterton, Seaton and Axmouth were big fishing centres. Around 1780, Teignmouth also had a large herring fishery. In 1840 the chief fishing ports of Devon were Brixham, Plymouth, Bideford, Ilfracombe and Combe Martin, Exmouth and Topsham, in that order. Brixham was sending fish to London, Bath and Exeter by the middle of the eighteenth century. By the beginning of the nineteenth it was the most noted wholesale fish market in the west of England.

In 1843 Brixham had 165 trawlers and twenty hookers and seiners at work. "Altogether this busy little place," writes W.G.Hoskins, "had more than 270 sail of vessels, comprising 20,000 tons of shipping, and employing about 1,600 seamen. The average weekly catch was about 150 tons but sometimes as much as 350 tons were sold on the Quay in a week. The Brixham fishing fleet returning under full sail in the evening was one of the great sights of the west of England, and a sight we shall never see again… The twentieth century saw profound changes in the methods of fishing, however, which have reduced the Devonshire fishing towns to a melancholy state."

Today her principal fishing ports remain Brixham, Plymouth and Kingswear, the main crab fishing centre of the United Kingdom. The weekly quantity of catch from Brixham, where 21,000 jobs are directly linked to fishing (a figure equivalent to one-third of the workforce of the town), was in 1995 just over 198 tonnes.. Fish harvested by its 45 beam trawlers included Dover sole, Lemon sole, cuttlefish, turbot, brill, plaice, whiting and scallops, valued at over seventeen and a half million pounds. In contrast, fishing from Plymouth is on a smaller scale. In the same year it was valued at only six and a half million pounds, largely because of its heavy dependence on mackerel, a less valuable catch. Unless the problem of quota- hopping is solved within the next few years, the Brixham fishing industry is almost certain to become more dependent on a less valuable harvest of non-quota fish—cuttlefish and scallops.

See page 182 for the story of a young Devon trawlerman.

THE BUILDING INDUSTRY

As W.G. Hoskins—the historian most quoted in this book—has observed, the building industry, with all its auxiliary trades and crafts, "must have been as important in the economy of Devon as the cloth trade, and possibly more important than the tin-working. One tends to forget its magnitude because it is scattered among small units, often single men, and because its products do not enter into the export markets, of which we have fuller records."

Nonetheless, on the subject of the most handsome of all English structures, the mediæval cathedral, some information has been recorded. The twelfth and thirteenth centuries, especially between 1160 and 1220, saw a tremendous religious revival. In Devonshire, the cathedral arose on the site of the old Exeter abbey; hundreds of parish churches were also being rebuilt in stone, and nearly a score of religious houses were founded before the end of the thirteenth century. At Exeter, Tiverton, Okehampton, Plympton, Totnes, Barnstaple, Lydford and Berry Pomeroy, major castles were being constructed, with smaller ones or fortified houses at Hemyock, Bampton, Powderham, Nutwell and Gidleigh.

A great deal of church building also took place from 1300 onwards. The quantities of stone and wood used, the quarrymen and foresters engaged, the masons, carpenters, tilers, stonecutters, basket-carriers, hodmen, bearers of hand-barrows, plasterers, mortar-makers, pavers, dressers, glaziers, painters and labourers, together with all the clerical administrators required to calculate the number of men and the materials needed in the construction of these buildings, is unknown. But it must have been extensive—as the following figures reveal.

In 1253, the accounts for Westminster Abbey suggest that the maximum number of workmen employed in the construction of a great cathedral was 428, the minimum was 100 and the average over the whole year 300. On a lay site, the number could be considerably higher where military interests played a part. When Beaumaris castle was built in Wales between 1278 and 1280, 1,630 workmen were employed: 400 masons, 30 smiths and carpenters, 1,000 labourers and 200 carters. Since all important mediæval buildings were constructed of stone, quarrymen and carters also played a significant role in the first phase of each new construction. In the three years which it took to build the last Cistercian abbey, Vale Royal in Cheshire, precisely 35,448 cartloads of stone were taken from the quarry to the site, over a distance of five miles. One cartload must have left the quarry about every quarter of an hour of every working day.

The widespread building activity of the years between 1400 and 1540 is evident everywhere one goes in Devon, to this day. The latter must also have supported a major industry, beginning with the quarrying and transportation of the stone and ending with the wood-carvers who produced the rood-screens, pulpits, bench-ends and roof-bosses of the churches, as well as the richly carved woodwork of the larger houses.

From the fourteenth and fifteenth centuries onwards an astonishing number of private mansions and houses were also under construction; many of these, like Saltram (see page 80), demanding skilled craftsmen for their embellishment. With their often luxurious ornamental plaster ceilings, carved staircases and overmantles, decorative metalwork, inlaid floors and other decorative features, the building and decoration of such houses must have provided employment for small armies of specialist craftsmen: joiners, plasterers, carvers and the like.

In the first decades of the nineteenth century there was a final flowering of great civic buildings—churches, speculative terraces and civic, naval and military buildings like Plymouth's Royal William Victualling Yard—before, broadly speaking, there was a relative breakdown of all the different and very specialist craft skills resulting from the introduction of mass-produced and prefabricated materials. Nonetheless, today, according to statistics provided by Devon County Council, over 14,000 people (3.9% of all those employed in Devon) continue to work in the construction business.

Builders working on the spire of Beaford church, rebuilt in 1802 and again in 1908-9, the date of the photograph.

THE GREAT WESTERN RAILWAY

Railways were the first major mechanical invention directly to affect most of the population; their arrival in the county produced the most far-reaching consequences in its history. They led to Devon's integration into the mainstream of national life, encouraged the migratory spirit, introduced mass-produced building materials and transformed the economy. Their coming also killed off many of the old market towns, such as Chulmleigh, South Molton, Ashburton and Crediton, which were by-passed or only served by a branch line at a much later date. The railways likewise killed the coach and wagon traffic trade and all the businesses that had depended on it—the inns and public houses, the saddlers and harness-makers, the blacksmiths and wheelwrights, the corn and forage merchants, amongst others. When, on 1st May 1844, the engine *Actaeon* pulled the first steam train to reach Exeter, it carried with it not only six carriages filled with excited passengers but the first tides of the triumphant modernism which was to banish from the county its ancient past: the ordered society of craft, custom and community.

In the decades leading up to this inaugural journey, virtually everyone had travelled by foot, on horseback, by horse-drawn vehicle or by boat—if, that is, they moved around at all. Local time, not Greenwich time, was still in use, and few national newspapers penetrated so far west. Devon had largely missed out on the Industrial Revolution: the vast majority of its workers still laboured adjacent to the place where they and their families lived. By 1860, much of this had substantially changed; most of the trends in evidence today had been established by then.

The story of the railways in Devon is unmistakably linked with one man: Isambard Kingdom Brunel (1806-1859), the greatest engineer of the nineteenth century and architect of the Great Western railway. As early as 1836, Brunel was surveying a route from Exeter to Plymouth, proposing to bridge the estuary of the Teign, passing near Torquay and from thence carrying a line across the Dart and through the South Hams country. The levels were favourable but the works would have been extremely heavy. The plan was therefore abandoned on economic grounds, in favour of the route which the main line now takes, following the east bank of the Teign to Newton Abbot, crossing the Dart at Totnes and then skirting the southern fringes of Dartmoor through South Brent, Ivybridge and Plympton.

It was in this form that the South Devon Railway was authorised. Brunel built his broad-gauge line from London via Bristol to reach Exeter in 1844, Teignmouth and Newton Abbot in 1846 and Plymouth in 1848. The

section between Exeter and Newton Abbot was the scene of his experiment with atmospheric traction (a method of propelling trains by compressed air) but the system was abandoned after it was discovered that of the £433,991 spent only £81,000 had been recovered. In the early years, the sea wall on the five-mile stretch between Dawlish Warren and Teignmouth and up the Teign estuary also caused great worry and expense (and continues to do so). Brunel's Royal Albert Bridge at Saltash, the last and greatest of his railway works, was opened in May 1859.

Meanwhile, other railways were under construction—to Crediton in 1851, to Barnstaple in 1854, to Bideford in 1855, to Tavistock in 1859, to North Tawton in 1865, to Okehampton in 1871, to Torrington in 1872, to Holsworthy in 1879, to Princetown in 1883 and Yelverton in 1885. By the end of 1947, when the Great Western ceased to exist and became British Rail, there existed a railway network covering most of the county bar its north-western corner and, of course, Dartmoor, but losses were mounting and line closures became inevitable.

The Great Albert Bridge at Saltash, by Isambard Kingdom Brunel. A lithograph by J. Needham, 1859.

NEW BUSINESS

In 1943, at a time when he was living at Dartington Hall, the artist Cecil Collins painted *Landscape with Hills and River*, a radiant portrayal of the valley of the Dart with its river rushing down between the trees and the rounded hills of that idyllically beautiful landscape. More than fifty years later, the landscape of the South Hams remains substantially unchanged, but tucked away in its folded hills a new phenomenon is arising: the existence of a growing number of resourceful people who have chosen to make a living on and from the land. These include blacksmiths, saddlers, thatchers, potters, furniture, wind-chime and jewellery makers, as well as producers of a wide variety of foods and drinks.

"You show me an area in the world which compares

The Sharpham Vineyard, Ashprington, near Totnes.

with the South Hams," says Mark Sharman, Director of the Association which has been set up to promote the variety and excellence of the area's food and drink. "Within five to ten miles of here, a huge variety of foods are being produced. You can find oysters and mussels taken straight from the Avon; venison from the edge of the moor; traditional beer from Blackawton Brewery; cider from Whitestone Farm, organically grown vegetables from Riverford Farm and, of course, wines and speciality cheeses from here on the Sharpham estate! Over the last five years," he continues, "attitudes to food have changed. For a long time people used to want the lowest possible price and at the highest possible convenience. Today there's a growing number who demand not only quality but knowledge of where it's all coming from. They want local produce and service. And they're not necessarily well off. Food transcends class quite well."

Mark Sharman is a vigorous, no-nonsense kind of person—a good example of the breed of entrepreneur that inhabits the South Hams. Thirty-nine years old, he is intelligent and highly skilled. He also lives—and thrives—in an area in which, by the conventional assumptions of our time, few monetary satisfactions are to be expected.. With a First Class Honours degree in Mining Engineering, Mark had every reason to anticipate a well-paid career. Instead, some instinct guided him to return to the place in which he had been born. In 1986, after a sojourn in Canada, he chose a job on the land—as an apple farmer on the banks of the River Dart. Two years later he was offered the job of looking after the vineyards and winery on the Sharpham estate; eleven vintages later he is still working there, but now as Manager of its family-based Partnership which includes a creamery and farm. Sharpham is a working estate with its own vineyard, winery, creamery and 120 acres of permanent pasture grazed by fifty Jersey cows. It is the latters' milk which is made into twenty tons of cheese a year: a Coulommiers type (Sharpham), a semi-hard type (Sharpham Rustic) and a Vignotte variety (Elmhirst), sold all over the U.K. The land is also planted with fourteen acres of south-facing vines, whose juices form the basis of Sharpham's four distinctive wines. Mark and his assistants produce 30,000 bottles a year. The winery is currently the county's largest and most highly acclaimed. Yet Mark is confident that there is plenty of scope for further expansion of the estate by increasing the herd, registering as organic, growing vegetables, and taking on more than the ten people currently employed.

"The only future for small farms is to diversify and add value in the manner we are doing here. Maurice Ash saw this as far back as 1981 when he planted the first vines, but it remains even more true today than it was then. The economics of modern traditional or small-scale farming are diabolical, and almost certain to get worse. I'm very attached to this estate and I want to see it prosper."

Mark Sharman inspecting the wines.

CHAPTER SEVEN:

Devonshire Characters

Let us honour if we can
The vertical man
Though we value none
But the horizontal one.

W.H. Auden

DEVONSHIRE CHARACTERS

In the introduction to his book *Devonshire Characters and Strange Events*, Sabine Baring-Gould says precisely what I myself wish to say in regard to this chapter. As he (most eloquently) expressed it: "In treating of Devonshire Characters, I have had to put aside the Chief Worthies and those Devonians famous in history, as George Duke of Albermarle, Sir Walter Raleigh, Sir Frances Drake, Sir Josiah Reynolds, the Coleridges, Sir Stafford Northcote, first Earl of Iddesleigh, and many another; and to content myself with those who lie on a lower plane… But even so I find an *embarras de richesses*, and have had to content myself with such as have had careers of some general interest. Moreover it has not been possible to say all that might have been said relative to these, so as to economise space, and afford room for others."

ROBERT HERRICK

The greatest poet to have been be born in Devonshire was Samuel Taylor Coleridge. He "sprang to light" in the vicarage of Ottery St. Mary on 21st October 1772, the youngest of ten children. His father, the vicar, was already fifty-three years old and his mother forty-five. They both adored him; according to his biographer, Richard Holmes, he was "a large, fat, greedy baby with a shock of unruly black hair, and huge grey astonishing eyes. 'My father was very fond of me, and I was my mother's darling—in consequence, I was very miserable.'" As a grown man, Coleridge made infrequent returns to his native county but never choose to live in it.

Of the poets who were born elsewhere but later settled in Devon, the most significant are Robert Herrick and, in complete contrast, Ted Hughes.

Little is known of Herrick's life. He was born in 1591 in London where, before going up to Cambridge, he was apprenticed to his uncle, a goldsmith and jeweller. At university he was ordained in the Church of England and in his late thirties took up a living in a small village near Buckfastleigh. From 1629, he remained at Dean Prior, writing poetry, conducting services and visiting his parishioners until 1647, when he was ejected under the Protectorate because he would not subscribe to the Solemn League and Covenant. All Herrick's poetry was written before this time. In that year he returned to London, where he resided until 1662, but under the Act of Uniformity he was reinstated at Dean Prior. He returned in 1663 and died at the age of eighty-three in October 1674. Robert Herrick (and his maid, Prudence Baldwin) are buried in the churchyard in unmarked graves.

*This engraving of Robert Herrick is a facsimile
of a seventeenth-century original.*

the county's sylvan genius and the old rural culture that went back to a time before the first Christians came to Britain. Herrick was a traditionalist, a Royalist and, in one sense, a pagan—a celebrant of the maypole, decorated with green boughs in honour of the gods of vegetation and fertility.

> I sing of Brooks, of Blossomes, Birds, and Bowers:
> Of April, May, of June, and July - Flowers.
> I sing of May-poles, Hock-carts, Wassails, Wakes,
> Of Bride-grooms, Brides, and of their Bridall-cakes.
> I write of Youth, of Love, and have Accesse
> By these, to sing of cleanly - Wantonnesse.

> I sing of Dewes, of Raines, and piece by piece
> Of Balme, of Oyle, of Spice, and Amber - Greece.
> I sing of Times trans-shifting; and I write
> How Roses first came Red, of Twilights, and Lillies
>   White
> I write of Groves, of Twilights, and I sing
> The Court of Mab, and of the Fairie-King.
> I write of Hell; I sing (and ever shall)
> of Heaven; and hope to have it after all.

Thus Herrick hymns the twilights of a Devon summer, its delicate scents and breaths of air, its stillness and the beauty of its shaded hedgerow flowers. Much as the carvers of stone and wood had celebrated its prolific vegetation in their pulpits, screens and capitals less than a few centuries before, so it is always to the summer's flowers that he returns—"to the lilly, the strawberrie, the rose, the violet, the primrose, the jasmine, the couslip and the daffadil."

Though Herrick served as Vicar of Dean Prior for thirty-four years, his poetry is full of sour and painful words about "dull" Devonshire, "the loathed West" and the "warty incivility" of Dean. In more than one thousand of his poems only one Devon place-name is to be found. Nonetheless his chief work, *Hesperides* (1648), a collection of some 1,200 poems, is deeply informed by

ARSCOTT OF TETCOTT

The oldest of the Devon gentry had their origin in the military class who served the great Norman lords in the late eleventh and the twelfth centuries. In return for the provision of military service when it was demanded, the Norman hierarchy gave them possession of their lands. At later periods, others rose to a higher social class through judicious marriage, hard work, a successful business enterprise, the law, or through no actual labour of their own but by the fortuitous purchase of a monastic estate at a low price. Marriage with the heiress of a neighbouring ancient freehold was often the greatest single cause of advancement.

Although the Devon gentry gave both local and national service—sitting on the Bench or 'representing' the district as an M.P.—and although they often built themselves delectable country houses (and celebrated themselves with no less delectable monuments and portraits), it has to be admitted that they rarely, if ever, made more than a limited contribution to the lives of the districts from which they presumably derived their incomes. Hunting, shooting, fishing, preserving game, entertaining their friends, managing their estates and generally looking to their own advantage and advancement were their principal occupations. Unselfish, unconditional generosity was a rarer pursuit.

Yet that was how it was. We must therefore honour the contributions that they made, amongst which I would unhesitatingly include their houses and parks. There are scores of these, but one of special strangeness and beauty is the manor of Tetcott, south of

A portrait of Black John, by an unknown artist. In the collection of the Royal Institution of Cornwall, Truro.

Holsworthy. With its rusticated atmosphere, picturesque roofs, severe stone and slate façade, lonely church and no less lonely park, it is one of the most evocative places in the county.

The last of the Arscotts of Tetcott was John Arscott (c.1718–1788), "well-nigh the last of the jovial open-housed squires of the West of England", wrote R.S. Hawker in his *Footsteps of Former Men in Far Cornwall*. I tell his story because of his striking individuality; he was one of the few squires (of whom I know) who was perfectly spontaneous and light of heart, loving and seemingly uninterested in the conventional.

Arscott was "benevolent to children and a generous and attentive host. . . an eager student of the laws of nature, and at the same time a devoted follower of the chase whether of the stag, or fox, or any other such beast." But, according to Baring-Gould in his *Devonshire Characters and Strange Events*, first published in 1908, he was also, and splendidly, "the patron of dumb animals". Hawker adds: "He lived like Adam in the garden surrounded by his animals and pets, each with its familiar and household name." "He was used to keep a toad on the doorsteps of his house with such care, that the hateful and loathsome beast, used to come out of its hiding place, when the master called it, and take its food on the table, before his astonished guests." Likewise he would "go in an old soiled coat into a wood where the ravens nested, and the birds would come down and settle on his shoulder, looking for the favours of a bountiful hand."

But Arscott's favourite was a figure, four feet high, "hump-backed and misshapen", a jester dwarf known as Black John, who lived from the middle of the eighteenth century to his death in 1788. "When the feast was over," Hawker recorded, "and the 'wrath of hunger had been assuaged'. . . the jester was called in to contribute by merry antic and jocose saying, to the loud enjoyment of the guests... Two of his usual after-dinner achievements were better suited to the rude jollity and coarse mirth of our forefathers than to the refinements of our own time." These were 'sparrow mumbling' and swallowing live mice. "The passage of the mouse was accomplished very often, amid roars of rude applause, down and up the gullet of the dwarf."

Black John's lair "was a rude hut, which he had wattled for a snug abode, close to the kennel." After his master's death in 1788, when "the agony of his misshapen retainer was unappeasable... he made for himself another lair, near the churchyard wall, and there he sobbed away the brief remnant of his days, in honest and unavailing grief for the protector whom he had so loved in life, and from whom in death he would not be divided. Thus and there, not long after, he died."

SABINE BARING-GOULD

If Tetcott is inextricably associated with the name of Arscott, and Dean Prior with that of Herrick, the same is no less true of Lew Trenchard: its squire and parson, Sabine Baring-Gould (1834-1924), lived there from 1881 until his death at the age of ninety, forty-three years later. He was born in Exeter, a member of the old, privileged, landowning class from whose ranks were drawn the members of the House of Commons, the officers of the armed forces of the Crown, and the lawyers, magistrates and judges who administered the law. Baring-Gould had

an unusual upbringing: between the ages of three and sixteen he travelled with his parents throughout Europe, spending less than three years in his native land. By the age of fifteen he could speak five languages, and had developed an ineradicable veneration for the past and a reverence for all things beautiful. Even at that early age he possessed a mind that ranged over a wide variety of subjects, as was later to became apparent in the novels, biographies, books of devotion and travel, reminiscence and studies of mythology, antiquities and folklore—in all over 100 volumes—that he wrote in his later years.

Baring-Gould studied at Cambridge, was ordained in 1864 and, as the curate at Horbury Brig, developed a mission of exceptional vigour. It was here that he wrote the words of his most famous hymns, *On the Resurrection Morning, Through the Night of Doubt and Sorrow, Now the Day is Over* and, in 1864, the most celebrated, *Onward Christian Soldiers*. It was here, too that he married Grace Taylor, who was later to bear their fifteen children. After the marriage, he moved in 1867 to Dalton in the East Riding of Yorkshire where, frustrated in his parish work, he was to turn his formidable energies more and more to writing. After a further year as rector of East Mercea in Essex, Sabine, being the eldest son, inherited the Lew Trenchard estate and returned to Devon in 1881 to take up the family living. He was forty-seven years of age.

At Lew Trenchard he developed a number of interests: writing books; tramping Dartmoor; collecting folk songs; restoring his church; improving the farms, cottages and houses on the estate and, as rector of the parish, setting himself the task of "the spiritual rousing of the people".

Each one of these could be described at length. His work as a pioneer collector of Westcountry folk songs, "the principal achievement of my life", has been

St. Peter's, Lew Trenchard, between Okehampton and Launceston.

described already (see page 127), but his work as an antiquary was also of consequence. In this capacity, he was the first to prepare a detailed report on the then almost completely unrecognised antiquities of Dartmoor. Everything about the moor then fascinated him: the traces of the mediæval tin workers, the ancient stone crosses, the legends, the flora of bog and upland and the simple life of the moormen. He wrote about them all in *A Book of Dartmoor, A Book of the West* and *The Transactions of the Devonshire Association*, of which in 1896 he was President. It was, he said, "that region I love best in the world." He also studied architecture, folkways and the byways of mediæval literature.

Despite the somewhat undirected character of Sabine Baring-Gould's labours, he was one of the last of the great line of English country parsons. The richness of his life, its indefatigable fertility and broad range of interests remain an inspiration today.

HENRY WILLIAMSON

Henry Williamson, though born in Brockley, Lewisham, lived and worked in North Devon for the greater part of his life. As a young man of nineteen immediately before the First World War, he had spent a brief holiday in the village of Georgeham, north of Barnstaple. Enthralled by its wild, unspoilt character, there and then he vowed to return.

The diary entries for this visit start on 16 May: "Sparrowhawk & 2 missle thrushes in the field, Barn owl in cottage roof, 'Cob', Nightjars reeling. Cuckoo on gate." Such observations were to form the basis of his books.

During the war he served as a soldier on the Western Front and participated in the Christmas Truce of 1914; it is on this period that five of the fifteen volumes of his novel sequence, *A Chronicle of Ancient Sunlight*, were to be based.

After 1918, Williamson worked for a brief period as a journalist in Fleet Street, but with his first novel, *The Beautiful Years*, accepted by a publisher, he made a decision to make his living as a full-time writer, and moved to Georgeham in 1921. "I am now in Devon," he wrote. "I've left London; all my eggs (egos) are in my one basket of literature; I've got £12 in the bank. Meanwhile I work. Today I heard about thirty linnets singing in a hedgerow, and their song was sweet." From this period sprang the inspiration for his *Village Tales*, with their unerringly accurate description of the now long-vanished life of Georgeham and the surrounding countryside.

In 1927, Henry Williamson wrote his most famous book, *Tarka the Otter*. To obtain accurate information he

Henry Williamson outside Skirr Cottage, Georgeham, 1921. He named the cottage after the calls of barn owls in the space under the thatch.

followed the local hunt, the Cheriton Otter Hounds, tramped over every foot of Tarka's 180-mile long journey from the tip of Dartmoor to Exmoor and the spectacular North Devon coast—an area of 500 square miles. In search of perfection, he rewrote the manuscript at least seven times over a period of three or four years. The author's seventh book, it was published in 1927, praised by Thomas Hardy, and awarded the

Hawthornden Prize.

After Henry Williamson's death in 1977, Ted Hughes gave an address in which he related that at the age of eleven years, he had read *Tarka the Otter* and "it entered into me and gave shape and words to my world, as no book has ever done since. I recognised even then, I suppose, that it was something of a holy book, a soul-book, written by the life blood of an unusual poet... It is not usual to consider him as a poet. But I believe he was one of the two or three truest poets of his generation."

In 1929, Henry Williamson and his family moved to a cottage called 'Swallowfield', three miles north-west of South Molton, where they lived for ten years. Here he wrote *The Children of Shallowford* and *Salar the Salmon*. During the Second World War he moved to Norfolk but returned to North Devon in 1948, remarried, and lived both in his writing hut in the Field he had purchased at Ox's Cross above Georgeham, and sometimes in Ilfracombe, for another twenty-nine immensely productive years. It was during this period that he concluded the cycle of novels that are sometimes regarded as his greatest work, *A Chronicle of Ancient Sunlight*, which chart the life of Phillip Maddison and his family and the way of life of England from 1893 until about 1953.

Williamson (whom I met on a number of occasions towards the end of his life) was a complex, difficult and controversial character. His domestic arrangements were fraught, his support for Hitler and Oswald Mosley wayward, and his life self-centred. Nonetheless, he remained true to himself, to his imaginative world and to his vision of England. Few have driven themselves so unremittingly; few have written so many compelling books.

IVOR BOURNE

If, as Hoskins writes, "the history of the farm labourer is almost unknown"—and in the early sixteenth century, about a third of Devon's rural population belonged to that anonymous class—the small farmer's story, if better documented, remains still relatively unstudied and unknown. Nevertheless, since the land of Devonshire has been cultivated by one method or another for at least 4,000 years, the personal testimony of its farmers is of considerable significance. I therefore count myself fortunate to have known one, Ivor Bourne, whose experience cannot have been all that different from that of his nameless forebears.

He was born in Witheridge, south-east of South Molton, in 1927, in a house in which his mother had been born and later died. At the age of eleven he visited his father's sister in the village of Beaford some twenty miles away. Originally intended as a short holiday, he stayed on, not only after the latter's death, not only after he had left school at the age of fourteen in 1941, but until his retirement from full-time farming forty-four years later.

In the first instance he worked for, and lived with, his uncle, on the latter's twenty-acre holding. It was here that he learnt and practised farming at first hand. He learnt the preparation of the land; the sowing of the seed; the harvesting of the corn; the care, feeding and milking of cows; the nurture of sheep; the growing of vegetables; the layering of hedges and the hundred and one other tasks that need to be done to run a successful farm. Here, too, he learnt that farming was not just a

way of earning a living, but a complete way of life.

There were then in the parish eight farms: all small, all sharing a common culture and a common place: Mount Pleasant, Cann's, Abbots Hill, Hole, Towell, Reeds, Philip Heard's and the Mill. But whereas most of these varied in size from about forty-five to eighty acres, and each kept about half a dozen cows, a few beef cattle and perhaps ten to fifteen sheep, the same parish now possesses only two farms: one of about 500 acres, the other of perhaps 300. The number of farm workers has commensurately reduced, from thirty-three to two. Ivor tells me that of the working farms that existed when he took up farming, only about a third have subsequently survived.

At the age of forty-four, Ivor and his wife Freda purchased the farm from his uncle, who had retired. Starting with thirty-three acres, he built it up to a hundred. By dint of hard work—rising at 5.30 am and often working a fifteen-hour day—he learnt its every corner,

its every slope, its every tree, and to recognise every cow (each one individually named) as intimately as he knew the faces of his daughters. And by his own account, there was always plenty to do: forty cows to be milked twice a day, 500 chickens and twenty beef cattle to be fed and nurtured, seven acres of corn to be sown and harvested. He grew kale, potatoes, Brussels sprouts and other vegetables to supplement the family's income, and went on a milk round—socially enjoyable, but taking up two and a half hours of his time every day. Freda was no less preoccupied with the work of the farm and household. To her fell the job of feeding the poultry, bottling the milk, washing the bottles (by hand), running the house and bringing up a family.

But the work, however arduous, was never dull. There was, he insists, a great deal of satisfaction in the variety and skill opportunities of everything he did—"laying a hedge, making a corn rick, playing cricket. Just the joy of doing something and knowing that you've done it well, as well as possible." I have, in fact, never once heard either Ivor or Freda complain. Their demeanour has been consistently unhurried, cheerful, generous and neighbourly. So much so that almost from the moment I met them, I recognised that I had glimpsed the real, the timeless Devon, a Devon still with us but fast diminishing.

This is not to say that this family was in any way unique. Many farmers and rural workmen—wheelwrights, saddlers, ploughmen, and the like—have possessed something of the same integrity, the same love of nature, the same unworldliness, the same absorption and modest pride in their work and delight in its small ordinary satisfactions. He told me how on a Sunday morning it was once common for a small number of men to inspect the furrows of any newly ploughed field. It was a gesture of friendship, solidarity and respect but woe betide those who failed in the estimation of the group's judgement. Work for them was more than a wage earned; they also knew the satisfaction of continuous creative work.

After we had chatted for a morning, I had to leave for home. But, no, he said, I must take some onions. We went to fetch them from a shed. Observing the great piles of split oak, I asked him why he and Freda needed quite so much wood. I should have guessed. "For the old folks in the village," he said.

CLIVE BOWEN

Clive Bowen was born in Cardiff in 1943. With the intention of becoming a painter, he studied painting and etching before moving to North Devon in 1965. It was there and almost by accident that he found himself taking up the craft of pottery, first with a four-year apprenticeship with Michael Leach and then as a production thrower working for the old firm of C.H. Brannam Ltd. in Barnstaple. In 1971, at the age of twenty-eight, he felt sufficiently assured to set up on his own account, and did so by borrowing the money to purchase a small agricultural property outside the village of Shebbear. It was here that he built his first small wood-fired kiln (out of scrap bricks from a local power station), with a capacity of 30 cubic feet. Five years later he constructed a double chambered kiln with a total capacity of over 400

cubic feet; it can hold up to a thousand pots, take up to five days to pack and is still in regular use. During its twenty-four hour firing period, the kiln is stoked with wood obtained from the local sawmill.

The choice of local materials is consistent with his vision, and his vision is of the district in which he has chosen to live. The clay he uses—red earthenware—comes from Fremington, as does the North Devon technique of slip trailing using different coloured liquid clays, combing and *sgraffito* decoration (see page 98 for further

details on North Devon pottery).

Early mediæval English ware in general, and North Devon pottery in particular, are, in fact, Clive's constant inspiration. Their robust vitality, practicality and unself-conscious nobility are the qualities he most seeks to emulate in his own work. His is an aesthetic of authenticity in which the specialist's divisions between work and life, and art and work, are consistently ignored. Little wonder then that his richly sensuous yet practical ware is somehow more than good art. His charges are consistently modest because he wants his pots to be used. They belong to the larder and the kitchen rather than the collector's cabinet. He exhibits them all over the world but takes pride in making ridge tiles and chimney pots commissioned by local builders.

Clive, of course, never designs on paper what he intends to make. He never puts his life under the rule of abstract ideas or monetary values, nor is he attracted, as so many of us are, by the pursuit of originality. What he seeks is "use in beauty and beauty in use", that mixture of beauty and utility whose loss Shakespeare lamented in *Henry V.*

He lives with his wife Rosie and their children, surrounded by animals and wild, wooded countryside: old oaks, springing copses and empty lanes. Their lovely natural garden and neat allotment supply most of their daily needs. The pottery is a step or two from the house. All this is what Eric Gill would have called, a "cell of good living" in the Devon countryside. Few have chosen to live as he has, at the crossroads of a vital paradox: by having little, to have much; by living frugally, to live abundantly.

SHEILA CASSIDY

It is arguable that Sheila Cassidy is as well known as any of my other 'Devonshire Characters', but it is not the reason which attracted me to include her in this

book. I wanted her participation because the qualities which have characterised her life–dedication to purpose, fulfilment of promise, ideals of service, humour and creativity–have so strong an appeal for me.

Her mother was English; her father an Australian who came to England on a Rhodes scholarship. Later he served as the senior lecturer at a RAF electrical wireless school in Lincolnshire, where Sheila, the youngest of their three children, was born in 1937. At the age of eleven her parents left England for Australia, establishing a small poultry farm on the outskirts of Sydney. It was during these adolescent years that she received both her calling to medicine and to the service of God. "I had no doubts that this meant a life devoted without reserve to the service of God, and that this in its turn meant the renouncing of marriage, of medicine and of my liberty." Sheila has never married; she has also followed her vocation for healing, studying medicine first in Sydney and from 1958 at Oxford, where she qualified in 1963. "I love mending things," she told me. "Anything broken; broken people, maybe."

After Oxford she joined the Casualty Department of the Leicester Royal Infirmary, working between sixty and eighty hours a week. By 1971, although she had not lost her early love for medicine she had become disillusioned about the way junior hospital doctors were then expected to work.

So, seeking to escape the demands of the British medical rat-race and further her desire for operative experience, she sailed for Chile in December 1971. In Santiago she worked as a resident in internal medicine. She also experienced the heady months of the left-wing

Sheila Cassidy outside the walls of her House of Torture, the Casa Grimaldi. The photograph was taken on a later visit to Santiago.

government of Salvador Allende and the military coup which overthrew it. Here, too, she saw the poverty of millions; made deep friendships with numerous Catholic nuns and priests and served at the Posta, an emergency hospital providing the only source of medical aid for the thousands of the city's shanty town dwellers. "I was weary and harassed and swamped with demands and yet at the same time alive and aglow as never before."

Then on 21st October 1975 she experienced what could be called the defining moment of her life. A priest asked if she would be prepared to treat a wounded political fugitive fleeing from the secret police. "Without hesitating I said 'Yes', knowing quite well that this might mean the end of my work in Chile. It was not my place to judge this man but to treat him." Soon after she did so, she was arrested by the security forces, stripped, gagged, tied to a bed and given electric shock treatment to force her to reveal the whereabouts of her patient, and who was harbouring him. After this, she was placed in solitary confinement and imprisoned in the Casa Grimaldi, one of the three Houses of Torture in Santiago. Her three weeks in solitary confinement and five weeks in a concentration camp are described in *Audacity to Believe*.

In December 1975, she returned to England. Aged 41 and still convinced by her calling to the monastic life, Sheila decided to fulfil the summons she had felt as a girl of seventeen: she lived first in a cottage in the grounds of Ampleforth Abbey, then within the walls of an enclosed order, with the idea of eventually starting her own. With hindsight it is difficult to understand how this boldly spoken, dynamic, ambitious, intuitive, richly creative yet depressive maverick, could have survived for as long as she did—seventeen months—within the restrictive disciplines of a Berdanine convent. "I wasn't convent material," she has acknowledged. "I'm a loner and unsuited to community life." At all events she was miserably unhappy and was asked to leave. Nonetheless, not so easily defeated, Sheila then tried again; for six weeks she lived as an isolated hermit in a caravan on her brother's Devon farm, and failed again. Looking for work, she found it at the local hospital and within twenty-four hours realised she was back where she belonged. "I realised my primary calling was and is to medicine." she told me. "I believe people are called to do certain things. It's not always easy to discern what these things are. But for myself I know that it has to be

a close personal relationship with God and the service of other people."

In 1982 Sheila was offered a job as Medical Director of a new Plymouth hospice for the terminally ill, which has since moved to larger premises. At the age of forty-five, she had found her true *métier*. "The work, preparing half a dozen people to accept that their cancer was terminal, and facing another six who would die each week, was sort of hard. With only twelve more days or hours to live there's no time to mess about with surnames and small talk: you just get on with loving."

After twelve years at St. Luke's, she became the Palliative Care Specialist in Plymouth General Hospital, and then moved to another job to pioneer a new service in the interface between cancer medicine and psychology, called psychoncology, Today she works at Plymouth's Freedom Fields Hospital, as part of a team at a cancer drop-in support centre which she started, called The Mustard Tree. "I went into the convent," she says, "in search of a 'holier than thou', if you like, but I have found more love and more generosity in an ordinary medical hospice than I ever did in a convent. The hospice movement has rediscovered a way or style of loving which is very close to what Jesus taught."

But if this work were not enough, Sheila finds time for activities which engage her heart and mind: prayer, preaching, lecturing and writing. She is the author of eight books, including one about the journey of those suffering terminal illness, *The Loneliest Journey*, and another, *Good Friday People*, which looks at the reality of suffering. These have been written mostly at weekends in her inimitable Plymouth attic flat, whose windows face the sea. Here Sheila has found her sanctuary, her place of refuge, her 'safe space', where after a storm-crossed day working with "people who are in hell", she can unload grief, depression and despair and find solace not only in prayer but in her love for knitting, cooking, books, flowers and, not least, her innumerable teddy bears. "I know that I have somehow come home, have found a safe anchorage in the depths of the unseen God."

RODERICK AND GILLIE JAMES

Close to Dittisham, across the tidal creek and up a secret wooded path, there lies a close-knit group of buildings of beguiling loveliness. There is a house, a studio and, most spectacularly, a new oak barn. The studio is where Gillie James makes quilts the colours of Neapolitan ice cream; the timber frame barn is grander, sterner, more monumental, as befits the workplace of her husband Roderick, co-founder of the company that built this exhilarating structure, Carpenter Oak and Woodland.

I met Roderick when he was directing the Centre for Alternative Technology in Wales. Trained as an architect, he had married and moved there because its houses were cheap; Gillie and he had purchased one (no water, no electricity) and worked on it with the indefatigable vigour that still characterises their lives. "I even made its window frames," he says but without a trace of self-satisfaction. "It's a terribly fulfilling thing to use your hands, to make your own house".

In 1974 he became involved with the Centre for

Alternative Technology which had opened at nearby Machynlleth. It was one of those cases of the right person at the right time and place. Within a few months he was designing the site, directing thirty volunteers, and establishing everything needed for the first visitor centre of its kind in the U.K. Within a few years, it was attracting over 60,000 paying visitors a year.

After six fulfilling but utterly demanding years, Roderick and Gillie left for Gloucestershire, where they set about the creation of a different life. They purchased and converted a house, carved bird decoys, sold ships' models, while at the same time Roderick did consultancy work for a proposed National Energy Centre

for the Milton Keynes Development Corporation and, significantly in the light of later developments, "a little bit of selected architectural work". Seven years later the family—now including their three young sons—moved again, this time to the South-West: to Dittisham, close to Dartmouth. Roderick believes that they will never move again: it is the spot on earth, he assures me, that will be their final resting place. Sitting in the honey-coloured barn, surrounded by the evidence of recent work—an oak frame church for the monks of Elmore Benedictine Abbey, repairs to the fire damaged mediæval kitchen at Windsor Castle, major elements of the newly opened Hindu Temple at Neasden, an oak framed theatre for Bedales school and a house at Chappaquiddick in the States—I can see why they both enjoy fruitful and deeply positive lives, for they live in a setting of breathtaking natural loveliness and enjoy making things both useful and beautiful. "I love waking up and seeing the water moving," he says, "I love the sea and the beauty of the creek. And the fact that lots of our friends are both unconventional and unpredictable,

only adds to the richness of our lives in this part of Devon."

With a partner, Charles Brentnall, Roderick founded Carpenter Oak and Woodland Co. just over a decade ago. Wood, before its replacement by other materials, had always been used on an immense scale. The roofs of Westminster Hall and Winchester College, the tithe barns at Great Coxwell and Abbotsbury, and, for that matter, Ernest Gimson's design for the library of Bedales School (1920), were all constructed of oak—so how, they puzzled, could its use be revived? Could the oak frame be made applicable for contemporary use? They thought so, and formed a company to prove it—a task they took on with considerable success. The company now specialises in the repair of old oak frame buildings and the building and erection of new green oak frames for barns, offices, public buildings, roofs and conservatories. It employs 50 to 60 people, mostly carpenters, and operates from four sites.

The greater part of the wood that is used comes from indigenous oaks—unseasoned, green wood, whose settlement is integral to its nature and appeal. "I want that movement, that charm that comes from a building growing as you live in it. I like buildings you can extend, change, hammer a nail in. I like robust, lived-in places. We have no concern to make ridges dead straight, but neither do we make them intentionally crooked." One aspect of this feeling for the vernacular and organic is Roderick's sincere commitment to what he laughingly calls "the ecological and environmental spin". Yet, as a person of a robustly pragmatic character, he has always avoided the dangers of tying himself up in an ideological knot. Oak buildings are clad with stainless steel and organic carrots rejected in favour of 'ordinary' ones if the former are half-rotten or tasteless.

Nonetheless there can be no doubting the commitment to sustainability. Gillie and Roderick have planted 7,500 oak trees around their creekside home. "We enjoy the forest growing while we enjoy the house." He also makes a point of urging every one of Carpenter Oak and Woodland's clients to plant trees. The company provides each of its customers with eight oak seedlings so that in, say, sixty years, their descendants can build another barn.

In addition to his work for the company, Roderick runs an extensive architectural practice designing buildings based upon the oak frame. "We must return to a more responsive style of building," he urges. "One that accepts the idiosyncracies, the gaps, the joints, the odd corners and spaces; one that is responsive to the spontaneity and messiness of human life."

If the barn at Dittisham Mill Creek and the rambling visual charm of their adjacent house are anything to go by, Roderick has achieved his aim. "It is possible to build a dream," he told me, "and I want as many people as possible to be able to do so. That is what I feel I'm here for." And that, I felt, is what he had achieved for himself.

REG AND HAZEL KINGSLAND

In the forties, H.J. Massingham wrote a series of books in which he celebrated the lives and work of a number of Chiltern country craftsmen, including Samuel Rockall, the wood-bodger; William Youens, the basket-maker; H.E. Goodchild, the chair-maker; Perkins of Chearsley, the wheelwright; and James Pike, the waggon-maker. All of these, he argued, "represented that English tradition which produced Shakespeare and Lincoln Cathedral". Yet if these are long departed, it has been my good fortune to meet some of their successors. Reg Kingsland is one of them.

Reg was born sixty-five years ago, the son of a farm worker with ten children, at Well Farm in the parish of South Tawton. The family moved around in a succession of tied cottages: to East Ash (where his father worked with horses and did other jobs on the farm), to Cranbrook cottage, about two and a half miles from Moretonhampstead, and then to a further two farms and homes, all in a radius of twenty miles. He went to school in the same area, first to Whiddon Down County Primary, then to Chagford Secondary Modern, which he left in 1946 at the age of fourteen and without a single pass in any examination. Even today, by his own admission, he cannot properly spell.

Judged by the false accountancy of contemporary educational theory, Reg Kingsland's schooling was a failure. Yet I have met few whose lives have been lived more usefully and contentedly. To encounter him and his wife Hazel in their neat Copplestone home, is to discover how much happiness can accrue from the simple

application of intelligent service to the nurturing of living things—animals, land, children and neighbours—without regard for the predatory appetites which rule most of our lives. "To be out of doors in touch with nature. To be able to grow something, tend something. Walk about the fields amongst the cattle and the sheep. That's all I ask for," he told me.

His life has been spent mainly on the land: hoeing, hedging, sowing, harvesting, feeding cattle, horses, sheep and pigs, milking cows by hand, and latterly performing self-taught miracles with machinery of all kinds. Reg was, it seems, especially fortunate in regard to his employers, yet I suspect that at least part of this success can be attributed to his qualities as a worker and his character as a man. "In those days we took it as it came. Most people fitted in and were happy with what they had to do. Everything was enjoyable. We worked long hours. We worked from seven in the morning until five

at night and on Saturdays until one o'clock. I don't know how we got through all the work but we did. And yet, you know, there was always time to talk. There was always time for recreation. Before I was married it was rabbiting, especially on Boxing Day, dancing, walking, motor bikes and growing vegetables." It sounded so attractive I felt obliged to question him about the less desirable aspects of his work, heavy rain for instance. "Oh! we just put tatty bags around our knees and over our heads and got on with the job. And when these were soaked we exchanged them for dry ones."

Aged forty-five, Reg Kingsland left farming, but not by choice—the man for whom he had worked for eighteen years had been obliged to move to another farm, but one without an agricultural cottage. (There has always been a great shortage of farmworkers' cottages in Devon, a situation which continues to the present day.) Thereafter Reg worked as a groundsman and peripatetic worker with a gang mower, being employed by the County Council for a further twelve years. In 1991 he was made redundant and spent the last few years up to his retirement as a gardener-handyman with a small Crediton firm.

Hazel, his indispensable partner, has lived a parallel life. Her parents were smallholders near the village of South Zeal; they possessed ten acres of grassland and three cows. Her father was a quarryman; she helped her mother with the milking and learnt domestic skills. But Hazel attended different schools: South Zeal Primary and the old Okehampton Senior, leaving the latter at fourteen but staying on at home before marriage at twenty-two. Hazel is not a garrulous person, but she positively flowered when describing the pleasure she used to feel when, as a girl, she helped collect the bracken from the moor in a little donkey-driven cart (it was used for winter bedding for the cows), and how she cried when the cows were sold.

After her marriage, children followed: a daughter and two sons, all of whom still live in the vicinity. Their daughter lives a few miles away at Bow; the sons, one in Crediton, the other at Lapford; none working on the land. From the way she talked about her family I could see that Hazel herself had been a wonderful companion and the creator of a caring and supportive environment: a good mother and home-keeper. Love, for her, though unspoken in our conversation, was an intimate and ordinary daily occurrence. It was the ground of her life. "Married lives are very important," she affirmed. "Wherever one of us has gone, the other has gone." Nowadays such affirmations for home and family are increasingly, and misguidedly, maligned. Acts which make ever more particular and precious the places and creatures where we live are surely to be preserved. In Hazel, one could but admire the results of a life of such selfless devotion.

Twice a year the family—all fifty of them—go together for an extended walk, and at Christmas they celebrate their togetherness. Reg has been to London once, Cornwall only four times. "I see all the things I want to see in Devon," he told me. "the countryside, the beauty of it, up to Belstone Tor and look around. What more can you want?" I sensed that Hazel agreed.

JAMES AND SANDY LOVELOCK

Previous articles about James Lovelock, the atmospheric chemist and inventor, have invariably ignored his wife. I cannot do that. To celebrate one and ignore the other is a distortion of their mutuality. "I don't think I've been as close to anyone as Jim," she says. "Nor have I. It's an affair of dynamic close coupling," he retorts. They are sitting together on the sofa opposite me, fingers intertwined. Jim is seventy-eight and Sandy a sparkling fifty-eight.

So if Sandy's story will be briefer than that of her husband, as a person she is no less impressive: an attractive woman, assuredly and even serenely equal to the demands and opportunities of her new life. In fact the more one ponders their marriage—its coming so late in their lives, its meaning to each of them, all that it has led to—it is obvious that Sandy has played an equal part.

She comes from America, where she studied English Literature at the University of Missouri before teaching for eleven years in schools in Florida and St. Louis. In 1973 she visited this country for the first time. "I fell in love with England then," she says. Later she married an Englishman, and the couple returned to London six years later. Here she developed her enthusiasm for music and the theatre, for both of which she expresses a characteristically exuberant delight.

She and Jim met in 1988 and fell quite suddenly in love. "We just seemed to come together. I took his arm. It was very, very strange. We'd only met two days before." At the time he was approaching seventy, and had been married for 46 years. His wife, Helen, was a serious invalid, about nine months from dying, and though neither he nor Sandy knew it, the latter's husband David was to die of cancer two years later. "The situation was thoroughly unfavourable," he told me, "what we did was wrong, but somehow from it has come a wonderfully productive nine years." After the deaths of their two spouses, the couple married on Valentine's Day 1991 and moved to their present home, an old Mill in a beautiful location in the remote countryside of West Devon.

Jim had purchased it with fourteen acres in 1977. Now, enlarged to thirty-five, the house is surrounded by a growing forest of native trees, going back to nature. "Leave it alone," he says. "Humans have done too much already." Non-interference is a central tenet of Gaia Theory, the theory of life with which his name will be forever associated. The story of his search for and discovery of this being is told in his first book, *Gaia: a new look at life on Earth.*

Gaia (at least for an ignorant non-scientist like myself) is a relatively simple, if revolutionary, idea—simple because of its comprehensive holism; revolutionary because it rejects the myth of humanism. It proposes that the earth and all its living matter behave as if they were a single living entity. "The earth's atmosphere," he tells me, "has always adjusted its composition so as to keep the surface comfortable for life. This is an emergent property of Gaia and more than could be expected of its constituent parts." So if Gaia exists, then we and all other living things are but parts of a vast being with the power to maintain our planet as a fit habitat for life. Gaia was the name given by the ancient Greeks to their earth goddess. Since the eighties it has become a name to describe a dawning awareness that humanity is neither superior nor apart from Gaia but an integral part of her.

But Jim's path to this comprehension, like Darwin's to *The Origin of Species*, was not a straightforward one; great ideas may come in a flash, but only to those who have prepared the way. In his case this involved the acquisition of three degrees—in chemistry, medicine and biophysics—and a career moving across the seemingly impervious borders of Medicine, Biology, Instrument Science and Geophysics.

Although Jim has worked for the Medical Research Council, as a Professor of Chemistry at Baylor University College of Medicine in Houston, Texas, and at the Jet Propulsion Laboratory, Pasadena, California on Lunar and Planetary Research—where the quest for Gaia began in earnest—for the last thirty-five years he has largely ploughed his own independent scientific furrow working from home.

"Writing is incredibly hard work. And my spelling is almost hopeless," he says. "But I can invent. I get great joy in inventing. Inventions just flow into my head all the time." In addition to inventing the microwave oven in 1955, he has written approximately 200 scientific papers and filed more than 50 patents, mostly detectors for use in chemical analysis. The most significant of these is the Electron Capture Detector, whose use made it possible to demonstrate the presence of CFCs in the atmosphere, the main cause of the depletion of the ozone layer. Its invention also led to the discovery of the ubiquitous distribution of pesticide residues in the natural environment—information which enabled Rachel Carson to write *Silent Spring* (1962).

Since 1974 he has been a Fellow of the Royal Society; he has been awarded seven Honorary degrees and is the recipient of numerous awards and prizes. These include the Volvo Environment Prize and, in 1997, the Blue Planet Prize. But if the reader has begun to suspect that Jim might be more super than human, nothing could be further from the truth. The fact is that he and Sandy are truly simple people. They are high-spirited but humble, intelligent but unpretentious, sophisticated but almost child-like—a quality that ensures his continuing ability to turn things on their heads. Thus they can live creatively, enjoy laughter and an intense and whole-hearted unity. Jim, it is true, is a gleeful iconoclast, a man of independent thought; Sandy, is also almost wilfully independent. But intuitively they live, like Gaia, as one harmonious organism.

It is probably because of this simplicity that it is so difficult to think of them as city-dwellers, yet Jim only moved to the country in 1956. It was to a village among the Wiltshire Downs, first seen on a bicycling holiday at the age of fifteen, to which he there and then vowed one day to return. "In the fifties," he told me, "the fields around Bower Chalke were just one riot of wild flowers. There were thirty types of wild orchid and virtually no cars. The novelist William Golding (who suggested the name 'Gaia') and I were the only intruders. The rural England of those days was coherent and idyllic—much as it had been for centuries. And then," he adds, "almost without warning, agribusiness came in. All of a sudden everything went. Meadows were destroyed, hedgerows ripped up, the little blue butterflies disappeared. The labour also left. The village was yuppified. Up to 1969, it was alright; after 1977, it was dead."

In that year, Jim moved west in search of a place with land, a place where the old way of farming had been sustained, and found both in the parish of Broadwoodwidger, where he continues to live. "The whole of rural Devon, the most amenable county in Britain, should be turned into a National Park." he suggests. "The quiet countryside is its greatest asset; the car its deadliest menace. In my youth the countryside was so good but much of it has been destroyed. Thank goodness for the stretches of undisturbed countryside that exist in Devon today. But how long will they last? How do we know we've a hundred years left?"

JAMES MARSHALL

Although he has lived for a decade in Devon, James's natural ebullience, extroversion and brogue place him as a northerner; despite massive homogenisation, regional differences still count. He was born in Southport, Lancashire, the fourth child of a wholesale tobacconist and confectioner who moved to Devon in 1988 to run the Welcombe pub. At twenty-six years of age, James is still a young man.

At school in Bude he did something which had important consequences for his later career: he undertook a two-week Job Experience course with a local thatcher. Always enjoying the outdoor life, he soon discovered that he and thatching liked one another so much that he decided to become a thatcher himself. In 1987, aged fifteen and a half, he left school to start a five-year apprenticeship scheme with the Rural Development Commission; in 1993 he was assessed as

the top thatching apprentice for the year, and in 1997 set up business in his own right.

"Ever since then," he told me with the engaging friendliness which defines his character, "the work has piled in. The demand is incredible. I'm booked up for months ahead." I asked him about the history of the thatcher, and was told how ancient a trade it was and how few thatchers were working in Britain today—a mere 600 of them, with about 60 in Devon as a whole, and only four of these in the north of the county. It was, he told me, considerably harder to make a living there than in the south or, say, in Wiltshire. "In those parts there will be no one thatching under the conditions I work in. Everyone thinks it's an idyllic kind of life but I can tell you in a wind it's the hardest job in the world. And in the summer you can get cooked alive."

Yet, for all its disadvantages, James is whole-hearted about his love for Devon and for his work. "When I think about it, the thought of moving back to the north fills me with horror. I belong here. I belong to Devon. I'll never move back. I like the pace. I like the simple humanity of it all. You can walk past anyone, anywhere. At the worst they'd say "hello", and at the best you'd be stuck with them for half an hour. I love the winter, too, when you can walk all day and see no one. The emptiness—you can get lost, you can drive round in circles, everything interwoven with little lanes and hamlets—yet however isolated you feel you're never deserted. You're never alone. People are everywhere ready to help. They make you a cup of tea; they welcome you. Everyone thinks that North Devon is an empty landscape but that's wrong: the fact is that everyone knows where everyone is and what they are all doing."

For his labour, James charges at a rate appropriate to the local area but, he says, an older, more experienced thatcher will charge between £800 to £900 a week. The average thatch, which can last from twenty to thirty-five years, costs anything between £3,500 and £5,000. He uses Devon wheat reed from Ashreigney and Copplestone, especially grown and harvested "exactly as it was", and employs it according to the peculiarly Devonian thatching style : plump and rounded to match the landscape and prevailing weather. "I always attempt to suit the local landscape and the buildings, rather than their inhabitants," he confesses. "It's the building you have to think of. I'm here to sell people what they need rather than what they want."

Despite his youth, James is immune from the worst infections of our time. He is assured and confident of his worth, but with a practical grasp of Thoreau's ideal of 'a life of simplicity, independence, magnanimity and trust'. He delights in the fact that everything he has ever bought has been paid for by his own hard work. "I look at the people of my age, working in high street shops and factories, and I see they're never going to achieve anything. They lack vision and pride. I've never wanted to be normal. I've never wanted to be average. I like going to work. Even if it's chucking it down I like achieving. In years to come, I want people to say this was done by James Marshall. In years to come I want people to say James Marshall thatched this roof. He was a good thatcher. He was someone to be relied on to do a good job. Please, John, don't be deceived: there's nothing humble about a country thatcher."

JOHN MOAT

John Moat was born in India in 1936. Three years later he was brought to England, to a valley between Buckfastleigh and Coombe on the southern fringes of Dartmoor. There, with his mother and sister (his father, a regular soldier, was killed in battle in 1942), he lived in a converted Mill near the house, reputedly the inspiration for Conan Doyle's *Hound of the Baskervilles*.

The landscape of his childhood was, he believes, haunted by a richness and a mystery which has stayed with him ever since. It was and is his valley of vision. "Devon, at that time, was a totally magical country. The countryside through which I rambled was a very, very powerful nature-place; a place, as it were, inhabited by the great god Pan." As a boy, like other happy young animals, John enjoyed to the very full the life of the senses. But there was also some unusual thing in him that made experiences memorable and lasting. "Let me tell you about a time when all that mystery crystallised into an experience I've never forgotten," he confides to me, his voice lowering to a confidential whisper. "My sister, a friend and myself—we were just kids at the time— were playing in a dingle on the edge of a wood. Suddenly we became aware that for some time we'd been listening to this sound, this high-pitched sound. . . first distant, but getting nearer and nearer, louder and louder. We looked at each other and saw the others afraid. Put our hands over our ears. And then we were running. . . for our lives. So the valley was a haunted place. But for me all of Devon's landscape is the most secretive, the most private imaginable. Mostly you can't see and can't know what secret world is over the hedge. You climb a gate, go to sleep in a field, and you know you are or have been prone to some enchantment. Something or someone has been watching you from the wood. . . Something in this landscape. . . I wonder; did it condition me, or did it match a predisposition? Yet I felt that because of my reverence, the landscape would always look after me."

Throughout the war, John lived at Brook Mill. "One of my earliest memories was of a bright light on the western horizon: Plymouth burning." In those years he spent hours in the woods and fields, in the bracken, along rivers, exploring by himself. Yet at the age of thirteen, moving to Hampshire, he became aware that something had irredeemably ended. Unsurprisingly, for the resemblances are singular, one of his favourite books

remains *The Prelude*, the poetic autobiography in which Wordsworth recounts the formative influence of his own country childhood in the wild mountain country between Windermere and Coniston. But if Wordsworth was to devote himself to poetry at the age of fourteen, it was not until after he had left Oxford that John experienced the quickening call of the word. He began to write, and it is as a poet, novelist, short story writer and painter that he has subsequently realised himself.

The human instinct to set down roots and return to the place of one's childhood is in some so strong that, with hindsight, it seems inevitable that John should have returned to Devon. In 1960, he found a house in the parish of Hartland, a house which provided the key to the way he wanted to live and needed to work. It was a mill, in a secret valley in earshot of the sea, possessed with, he says, "all the lineaments I'd most loved as a child: oakwoods, streams, meadows." Here he has lived with his wife, Antoinette, for almost forty years, sustaining a regular output of imaginative work: four novels, including *Bartonwood* and *Mai's Wedding*, six collections of poetry and a book of essays as well as a body of paintings, drawings and other miscellaneous work.

"To write," he says, "I'm not content even with a room in our house. I need my hut in the wood. All my study with writing has, I feel, been to learn to keep a secret, to move as deftly as possible by implication, to convey with an indefinable accuracy a little of the mystery of the valley in which we live." But if silence and secrecy are of cardinal importance, John is no recluse. He and his wife have a genius for friendship, and their house is often alive with guests and laughter. "For my sanity's sake," he tells me, "I need to get out of the closed crucible of the valley. And yet what I'm driven to do still stems from and is clarified by the secrecy of this landscape."

Does this relate to his founding in 1968 (with John Fairfax) of The Arvon Foundation, which still involves him in an endless round of meetings, or to his no less active work for the North Devon Christmas Festival? His response is characteristically affirmative. "With Arvon, or whatever other project I'm involved in, I'm interested in the undercover operation, moving independently of the shadowless scrutiny of the bureaucracy. So in the end the only service I'm committed to is making opportunities for others to be alive to their own imaginative life. In other words to tap the dark luminous potency of their own secret Devon valley."

ERNEST MOLD

Ernest and Jenny Mold came to Lynton in 1953, a year after the floods which left the village devastated and thirty-one people dead. He came as an assistant to the local doctor, Dr Nightingale, a man who in the war had done his rounds on a horse and rode with the hunt. Yet within six months Ernest and he were sharing the work; it became a partnership that lasted for sixteen years. Then, from 1969 until he retired in 1982, although Ernest retained overall responsibility for the practice, he shared the work with a new partner, Roger Ferrar. That work was the welfare of the people in an area of Exmoor stretching from Lynton to Blackmore Gate in one direction and Porlock Hill in the other. "Two thou-sand five hundred people depended on us completely, 24 hours a day, 365 days a year," he told me, with an understandable but muted hint of pride. "And until Dr. Ferrar joined me, for fifteen years I was on duty every night. I had very few weekends off. I've probably been in every house and cottage—and not a few cowsheds—within a radius of fifteen miles. You may wonder, John, why I've mention cowsheds but then I can't imagine you've seen anyone wounded by a cow."

Apart from in the remoter parts of Wales and Scotland, few can have dedicated their lives over such a long period of time—almost 30 years—in such a ravishing but isolated stretch of country: long, narrow, wooded valleys fingering their way deep into the moor, and thrilling plunges to the sea. But in this, as in other ways, Ernest Mold and his wife Jenny are exceptional. For her part, before the days of Health Centres, doctors' secretaries and the advent of the mobile phone, she never left their house in case someone needed the doctor in his absence. She would then telephone the farm nearest to where he might be, and ask the listener to run across the fields and wave down his car. Such unrecorded acts, however small in terms of portentous historical events, are nevertheless the solvent of a community.

To meet the Molds, it is apparent that they have lived fulfilling lives. There have been, as he tells me, many unsuspected rewards. "Professionally, I can't think of anywhere where I'd have had more clinical freedom— I could do everything I wanted to do, as I wanted to do it and when I wanted to do it. In fact I've done all sorts of things that elsewhere might have needed specialist attention, for example suturing the cuts that cooks and farmers have suffered from knives. I also did a minor operation on a boy whose eye had been pecked by a pelican at Ilfracombe zoo. I stitched it up and told his parents to return in a week. When they appeared there was nothing wrong with his eye."

Some of the best of Ernest's reminiscences are distinctive. This is especially true about those which took place during one of the historic winters of the last two centuries. In the year of 1962-3, snow fell on Boxing Day and continued falling for another two months. Lynton was cut off for six weeks; helicopters brought in bread, tractors carried the milk churns. With his partner suffering from angina, Ernest was alone. One midnight he

was called out to visit a farm a short distance from the main road. From here, he set off in the direction of the house, but if he knew where it should have been, find it he could not. "Surely it should be around here," he queried his companion. "Yes," the latter replied, "You're correct. We're standing by its chimney."

Apart from doctoring, Ernest has made a significant contribution to the life of his community. He is the Chairman of the Lyn and Exmoor Museum—a model of its kind—and been the moving spirit behind the twinning of Lynton with Benouville, near Caen. There are also few who know as much as he does about the flowers, the birds and, more particularly, the archæology of "our little bit of moor", on which, in his own words, he has become "a minor authority". For sheer recreation he sails a picaroona, a clinker-built boat unique to Clovelly and Buck's Mills, made for herring fishing.

I found my meeting with Ernest and Jenny a surprising joy. One cannot know them without rejoicing in their infectious human worth. Each was a necessary gift to the other. Both were thoroughly happy, at home with themselves and yet alive, without vanity, to the contribution they had rendered their community. They were people who understood that real wealth was more enduring than fame or the accumulation of worldly goods or power.

JOYCE MOLYNEUX

Although my 'Devonshire Characters' were never meant to be representative of Devon people, it was always my intention to include three skills essential to our welfare: those of the farmer, the doctor and the cook. So where better to find the latter than by asking one of Britain's most celebrated chefs if she would participate in my book? Without demur, and with characteristic friendliness, Joyce Molyneux agreed and we met in the *The Carved Angel*, the Dartmouth restaurant with which her name is inextricably linked.

Joyce's beginnings were modest. She was born in Birmingham in 1931, left school at sixteen and enrolled on a two-year Domestic Science course at the local Catering College. In those pre-war days, food (to put it at its politest) was basic, but the training she received was adequate for her first job: work in an industrial canteen at £2.90 a week. After twelve months she moved to a restaurant in Stratford-upon-Avon, *The Mulberry Tree*, where she worked six days a week for ten years, learning on the job. In 1959 she moved again, and in doing so took the most important step in her life: she joined George Perry-Smith (an outstanding restaurateur and an inspiring influence on the subsequent development of food in Britain) as General Assistant at *The Hole in the Wall* in Bath. Here the pay was better, and Joyce increased her repertory of skills. For if she found it "jolly hard work" it was also, in fact, an education in itself — "inspiring and satisfying". Towards the end of her twelve years at this restaurant, Joyce was not only in charge of the kitchen but had been taken into partnership with

George Perry-Smith and Heather Crosbie.

With the opening of *The Carved Angel* in 1974, Joyce found herself in charge of the kitchen with, as partner, Tom Jaine. Its success may have been rapid, but such acclaim never comes by accident. It demands exceptional skill, sustained dedication, the monitoring of consistent day-to-day standards, a vigilant attention to housekeeping and a continuous openness to all the food on offer—and a readiness to enjoy it. In all these factors Joyce Molyneaux has excelled. Her commitment to excellence, her feeling for materials and lack of personal ambition have made a visit to *The Carved Angel* a truly memorable occasion. *The Good Food Guide* consistently describes it as amongst the best restaurants in Britain.

Yet, like her person, Joyce's philosophy about her work is unpretentious. She regards food as not just an unimportant luxury, but as a celebration of life. She loves people, and likes to help them enjoy themselves as if they were guests in her own home. She regards her staff "like a happy family", but most of all, she enjoys food and loves cooking. "It can be done at a simple as well as on an expensive level with outstanding ingredients. I'm as delighted to work with mackerel as with the grouse which Robert Dart brings into the restaurant every early September. Do you know that when you come to pluck and draw them their crops are filled with pink heather flowers. Isn't that lovely and immediate!"

Her dedication to seasonal produce, most of it grown or reared locally, is an instance of her fidelity to the intrinsic quality of materials. In fact, Joyce scorns the preparation and cooking of food with whose origin she is not intimately acquainted. So Mark Lobb, a local fisherman who brings in the brill, the John Dory, the monkfish and the scallops; Manuela and Mike Lynn, who bring in the Dover soles and the cuttlefish; Robert Dart, who supplies the lobsters, the crabs, the pheasants and the game, are not only useful tradespeople but indispensable partners to her skill. Such attention to detail has always been one of the hallmarks of an exceptional artist, and for me she is one—and one of the finest in Devon. How else to describe a woman who takes the fruits of the earth and sea, and from them raises one of the simple acts of daily life into an art? "I want the best for everyone," she says.

CHARLES NAPIER

Charles Napier came to Drewsteignton, his parish sited high on the edge of Dartmoor, seventeen years ago. "I am a country parson and spend a great deal of time sitting in kitchens, drinking tea and talking about nothing in particular," he says smilingly. "Yet I know that God is always where reality is, and reality is a complex condition. God, too, is no respecter of persons. Nor is he only interested in those who say, Lord! Lord!"

Yet in truth, Charles, aged 69, is no starry-eyed evangelist. He has a questing, clear-minded yet tranquil intellect that enjoys wrestling with levels of reality vaster than those which interest the majority of his 1,200 parishioners. As such, he recognises that the Anglican church might be largely seen as a defunct force, "geriatric and middle class"; that it is a product of history and therefore both fallible and expendable. He admits that its members may also subscribe to its tenets to a very

The interior of St. Andrew's, Hittisleigh. With Drewsteignton and Spreyton, it was a parish for which Charles Napier had responsibility.

limited and convenient extent, that real belief is in profound tension with organised religion, and yet (and this is his wisdom) he is no less certain that "the Glory of God is the weight of the infinite mystery and power of everything that is." "The task," he believes, "is to see the mystery of reality, to see how everything relates to everything else and to do so in the knowledge of the full sacredness of all life."

But if Charles is critical of the Church of England, he is no less questioning of the assumptions which underpin our Western civilisation. He is quietly scathing about the "the masculine, colonialising and exploitative mentality which from the seventeenth century onwards has acted on the belief that the world is there for us to do whatever we want to do with it… That is what the Fall is all about—the arrogance of the human, the folly of believing that you can be as God, the belief that we have it in our power to define good and evil." It is this kind of thinking which has led Charles to pursue a path defined by a concern for social justice. Significantly, he was a founding member of the Devon Christian Ecology Group.

Within moments of meeting him I was sensitive to the subtlety of his mind, the peace and discernment of his nature and the seriousness with which he undertakes his ministry. Here, I could see, was no noisy extrovert, but a man in search of new paths to spiritual truth. For if Sheila Cassidy was in touch with an authentic feminine spirituality, Charles Napier was no less a pilgrim, in search of direct communion with the divine, for a relatedness to existence embracing both the timeless and the immediate present. He is someone who has understood that "the heart of real Christianity is to know how little you know about what needs to be known."

He was born in Eltham in south-east London in 1929, the son of an army officer; his background characteristic of what he described as "the usual pattern of 1930s middle class life": prep school followed by public school (Radley) which he left in 1947. Then there was Oxford, where he read history before experiencing "the rudest shock of my life"—two years as a conscripted soldier. In 1952, drawn by a commitment to the ideals of Christian unity, Charles entered the Roman Catholic Church, and after another eight years (four at the Jesuit Faculty in Louvain) he was ordained a Roman Catholic priest. Yet even as the deed was being done he was harbouring doubts about "the priesthood and the Church", doubts which were subsequently to take him back into the Anglican fold.

At the age of thirty, Charles had lost his spiritual direction; it was for him a period of trauma and exceptional confusion. Yet, characteristically, he set about his recovery in the sanest possible way: he gravitated towards the forgotten securities of his own spiritual and rural roots. "Though a soldier, my father was very much a countryman, who set up as a smallholder on his retirement. At that time, I was also attracted to the Reformation ideal of God in the ordinary—in the secular, in this-worldly issues." Putting his newly discovered rurality 'on hold'—it was in fact ten years before Charles was able to realise his dream of a country living—he moved in 1963 to a large, treeless parish in a suburb of Redruth. Apart from his years in the army, his curacy was another, second contact with the 'ordinary' world—and for him a life-enhancing one. At Illogan, he told me, "the evangelical Gospel gave me plenty to get on with." This sense of fulfilment in his parish work was enhanced by marriage in 1964.

Three years later, Charles was teaching Christian Doctrine at the London College of Divinity and St. John's College, Nottingham, where he stayed for seven years. But if he found both stimulus and pleasure in this work, his time there was to convince him that first and foremost he was not an urban dweller but, in his own words, "a rural animal". He and his wife therefore changed their centre of gravity. They moved west: to Warkleigh, an extensive parish of exquisite hidden country stretching from the very edge of Exmoor southwards to Umberleigh, with South Molton as its natural centre. Here, as part of a two-man team ministry, he travelled from church to church, conducted services,

taught the Faith, prepared parents for baptism, consoled the bereaved; and did so, I have no doubt, with the same grave dignity which characterises his life and work. "As a Catholic I had been trying to be something I was not. Returning to Devonshire, for the first time in my life I was being true to myself."

Charles, his wife and three children left Warkleigh in 1980. Inevitably, their next move was to a village where they were far from unknown: his father had lived in Drewsteignton from his retirement until his death in 1966, his father-in-law had been its rector through most of the sixties, and his 98-year-old mother lives in the parish today. After the doubts and traumas of his early manhood, his search to find roots, to be true to himself, the long journey of Charles Napier was reaching its conclusion. He had trusted the spirit in himself, cared for it and found that it had taken him home. To live in the countryside, to minister to country people, had been his long-cherished ambition. And now it was fulfilled.

Recently retired, he looks forward to years of quiet reflection and the continuing friendship of his many friends. He has the good fortune to be able to do so in a district and amongst scenery as beautiful as any in the world.

Sadly, Charles Napier died soon after the above had been written. For his funeral service, the Drewsteignton church was full to capacity.

ADY AND VANESSA NUTHALL

I was faced by a horse, three yapping but affectionate dogs, and plastic tractors on the lawn. Even before I met them, I had sensed the large, untidy, generous embrace of Vanessa and Ady Nuthall's lives. They live at one end of a large early seventeenth-century house (built on the site of an earlier twelfth- or thirteenth-century one) tucked away down a track in East Village, about four miles north-west of Crediton. Dira Farm is surrounded by fields, barns and all the paraphernalia of active agricultural work.

Ady and his younger brother Simon inherited the property and land (186 acres) from their parents in 1992; his mother had inherited it from her parents, who had arrived as tenants in 1931 and purchased it in 1952. The unbroken succession of generations now includes the Nuthalls' own children, a boy and a girl, who attend school in the nearest big village, Sandford, which Ady once attended as a young boy. From there he went on to the (then) Queen Elizabeth Grammar School, and Bicton Agricultural College, before working on farms. Ady returned to work alongside his father in 1979. In that year he was twenty; he has been at Dira ever since.

Apart from business and money worries, it was evident how much he enjoyed his work on and for the land. "We've got what we want," he told me. "The freedom, the independence. I can do what I want when I want to do it. In fact, I'm lucky to be born a farmer. But you know I'm more than a farmer; I'm the caretaker of this house and its land, which I've already willed to the children. I feel passionate about Dira and its fields—but the pressures to keep it all going have never been greater."

Like other farmers, Ady has been unable to avoid the strains inherent in the ever-increasing pressure to forsake the values of husbandry and assume those of finance and technology. On the one hand he faces all the paperwork, the regulations, the Government bureaucracy; and on the other, he has to live with the stress of an uncertain market for his produce. "Although I can't help loving it, a lot of the joy of farming has gone. There used to be a kind of romance about it, but efficiency is paramount now. It's more difficult to farm by your instincts. If it's not run as a business, you are finished and I'm not sure how good a businessman I am." Reflecting on his disheartenment, I wondered how many of Ady's contemporaries had also been forced to suffer the tragedy that is undermining the modern agricultural 'industry' as a whole: the tragedy of the nurturer being forced into the role of an exploiter, whose standard is efficiency, not care. "If I was a businessman and nothing else," he volunteered, "I'd flog the farm tomorrow, but I'm not and won't. Just something tells me not to do so. We love living here. It's home. It's our security. All the childhood memories…" To which I'd like to add Ady's obvious farming skills, his inborn and innate instinct to cherish and enjoy the ancient rule of neighbourliness and the traditional local culture. He shoots, fishes, sails, contributes to the local Round Table and is a serious and accomplished musician, playing trumpet and drums in a local rhythm and blues band. The Beagle Hunt regularly meets at the farm where, he says, the huntsmen devour chocolate cake and drink sherry on the lawn. He has been to London three times, and detests impersonal crowds.

"There's more to life than farming: to have everything but money is to have much." So although Ady is an unpretentiously 'modern' kind of man, when measured by the values of our commercial, urban culture, he remains an unusual one. Tied by inescapable bonds to the earth, he enjoys a rare feeling of belonging to his landscape and to his place in the local community. "If I walk into the pub," he told me, "I know I have an identity. 'Hallo Harry! Hallo Bill!' I say. I'm known there. I'm not a stranger. I'm one of the Nuthalls of Dira.'"

The other Nuthall—besides Simon, with whom Ady shares the farm work—is Vanessa, to whom he has been married for twelve years. Like him, Vanessa also enjoyed a rural background and went to the same Grammar school before she took a City and Guilds chef's course at Exeter College. For five years after their marriage they lived in East Village, but moved to Dira in 1991. Yet even before her two children were born, Vanessa had started

to develop her catering business—making and selling puddings to restaurants and pubs and catering for weddings—which now takes up much of her talent and energy. I asked here why she was prepared to work so hard. "I do it," she replied, "not only because it contributes to our relatively meagre income but because its helps to establish and maintain my personal identity. If I were the traditional farmer's wife—picking up the eggs and such like—I'd be, of course, an indispensable helpmate, but only in a supportive and essentially subsidiary way. As a caterer I am employing intelligence, capacities and skills that otherwise I wouldn't be able to use. I have created my own life in this way."

"Nonetheless," she adds, "for all the effort we put into our work, Ady and I are never going to make our fortune here. Yet there's so much to enjoy. I have only to wake up in the morning to see the riches we have been given. We love the house; the kitchen is lovely to work in—it's got two large windows through which I can look out and enjoy my roses. I like its space, its height, the fact that there's a lot of history attached to it. And then on top of the roses, my other passion is my horse, Miffy, and, of course, the local countryside. I ride out through the woods. There's a hare, a buzzard, a fox, the mist drifting through the valley! I can stand and look at things for ages. Without them, the catering and the children could get me down, but with them, I return refreshed. Then, too, there is the social side. My best friend lives around the corner, my brother is in Cheriton Fitzpaine and Ady's parents are just across the field. I have lots of long-established friends who'd come running if I was in a crisis. So though I'm not an old type of farmer's wife—I barely work on the farm—I am passionate about this place. I am rooted here. I hope to be here for ever." And she means it. Vanessa's investment of love and work, her commitment to household, neighbours and place, her enjoyment of precious things, reap immeasurable rewards.

PETER RANDALL-PAGE

At the bottom of the valley, balloons announce I am on track. A little further on, huge blocks of stone identify this as the home of a sculptor and, considering the early hour and all the comings and goings of workmen, that it is the home of a successful one. The room where we meet, an office stuffed with rolls of drawings, box files, volumes of slides and a computer, confirm the impression of well-organised creativity. But, for all that, Peter Randall-Page is not amongst the fat cats of contemporary art. He is a peaceful but energetic man with his own vision.

He was born in 1954, on the Kent-Sussex border. As a child, he enjoyed solitary walks into the local countryside, returning home with pockets stuffed with pine cones, shells, acorns, hazel-nuts and the like—the kind of material from which he continues to draw the inspiration for his present work. Yet, even as a boy, it was not just their surface beauty which impressed him but the relationship of their centres to their outsides, their volumes to their surfaces. Without the least awareness of his future path, Peter was already a sculptor, in thought if not in deed.

At sixteen, on one of his first trips abroad, he visited Paris. It was a decisive moment. The revelation was the studio of Constantin Brancusi, which opened his eyes not only to the possibilities of a life of dedicated purpose to art, but to a form of sculpture derived from nature. Back in England, he began to carve in wood, "reducing forms down to their essential essence".

At Bath Academy of Art, at Corsham, he continued to carve, and, at the same time, admiring the work of the great Japanese-American sculptor Isamu Noguchi, decided to correspond with him. The latter gave him helpful encouragement, as did the English sculptor Barry Flanagan, with whom Peter worked after leaving

Corsham in 1977. Further evidence of his dedicated path towards form came from his decision to 'apprentice' himself to two very different sculptural traditions. At first he worked for a season as a restorer on the great body of thirteenth-century sculpture on the West front of Wells Cathedral: "The importance of this work to me was enormous. The drapery carving was superb." Then (with the help of a Winston Churchill Memorial Trust Travelling Fellowship) he spent seven months studying stone carving and the techniques of triangulation at Pietrasanta, near Carrara, whose famous marble quarries had added to the lustre of ancient and Romanesque Rome, and to the work of Michelangelo.

Aged twenty-six and now certain of his future, Peter returned to England to set up shop as a carver in London, where he slowly acquired a reputation for his site-specific work. After twelve years, he and his wife Charlotte decided to move, and move they did—to a location far from the centre of the so-called art world,

but more in keeping with Peter's intuitive feeling for the natural and organic. In Devonshire, they settled in an old building with enormous barns, in easy reach of the nearest village, Drewsteignton. "I don't imagine ever leaving here," he confesses. "I love the hidden intimacy of the local landscape—amongst so much verdancy, you are aware of being in it, not on it. Everything here is wet and mossy and growing. Round every corner there is always something new to discover."

Like butterflies around a Buddleia, Peter and his sculpture seem to belong to this place. At the former mill he has created a whole series of organic forms, works rich in nuance—now clear-sightedly naturalistic, now evocatively ambiguous—which, if not specifically Devonian, are as rooted in the local countryside as the leaf carvings in the chapter house of Southwell Minster. He has created sculptures that belong to nowhere but the place for which they were conceived. "The things I find least interesting," he explains, "are illustrations of verbal ideas. Sculpture isn't an appropriate tool for making social and political points. But it is uniquely good at dealing with a particular form of human experience—as an object of meditation, something absolutely itself in an irreducible way. Something that hums."

That 'humming' is in evidence in all his finest works: it can be seen, for example in the split-boulder piece located at Broomhill Point, Derwentwater, Cumbria, or, in an urban context, the sculptural fountain in red and black granite for St. Ann's Square in Manchester. It is no less apparent in the five works that Peter has made in, around and for his own parish—works originally commissioned by the environmental group Common

Ground as an integral part of their 'Local Distinctiveness' project.

The commission demanded that the sculptures should be created on publicly accessible land and give expression to the local countryside and its human community. "First, I made a little carving in Ashburton marble and positioned it a few yards from where I live. Then I called a public meeting to introduce the idea. About 120 people turned up but there was a lot of skepticism. Then I walked the parish footpaths, negotiated with landowners interested in the concept and finally completed five pieces. In the end, the Parish Council became so supportive that they asked me to redesign the village's public garden. It's the way I feel most comfortable working. I was never altogether happy in London and the specialist art world that flourishes there. But here I couldn't be removed from everyday life. I had to embrace the local community and I've loved it. It's been an amazing experience."

Peter is a fortunate man; his life, with all its integrated parts and concerns, is fully realised—one organism, so to speak, in imagination and act. He is fulfilled in the work he enjoys doing and in making a living by doing it. "I live and work here. I invest my whole life here. I employ people and am part of the local economy. Yes, this isn't a farm any more but at least its a working place. All I believe one can do is to try to do one's best, to do good things."

ANNA ROBERTSON

In every village, every town, every city, there is always someone—and often many more than one—who works on behalf of the community. It may be manning a telephone for the Samaritans, providing meals-on-wheels for the housebound, raising money for a playgroup, sitting on the committee of a local charity, or contributing time and skills to any one of the multi-

plicity of voluntary organisations which exist to better the lives of the local citizenry or their environment. Without their contribution, Devon would be radically depleted of much that makes it such an attractive county in which to live. One such is Anna Robertson, who works on behalf of the Devon Branch of the Red Cross.

Anna was born in Sussex in 1947. Her father was in

the Fleet Air Arm, RNVR; her family (with some Scottish ancestry) were mostly doctors, magistrates or members of the church—people who took it for granted that they should contribute some time to public service and charitable work. "Ultimately, such work is a natural duty," she told me. Anna went to a boarding school, Queen Anne's, Caversham, before spending a year in France at the University of Grenoble, studying the language. Returning to this country, she worked for the literary agency A.D. Peters, the publisher J.M. Dent and, after a year or two, *Reader's Digest* magazine, where she ran the Small Features Department—and did so, I don't doubt, with the efficiency, enterprise and dynamism she subsequently brought to her extensive voluntary work. Yet the persona of the successful business woman must always have disguised a winning heart of gold.

In 1969, aged twenty-two, Anna married, and with her husband Tim moved to Worcestershire, where they started a family. Their first child was a girl, Chloë, born in 1971; their second, Gemma, was born in 1974, and their son, Sam, arrived in 1982. From a busy office overlooking Berkeley Square she adapted to the quieter life of a thatched cottage with a view of the Malvern Hills—and so relished the rural life that when her husband's career move was imminent, they decided to avoid the fate of the London commuter, and stay in the countryside.

The choice was Devon, where Tim had been offered a Directorship of the clay-producing firm Watts, Blake and Bearne. Here, they first lived at Haytor and then at Lustleigh, where they have remained for twenty-one years. It was also at Lustleigh, while her husband was

away from home travelling for the company (and in the process increasing its export market from eight countries, mainly in Europe, to over eighty worldwide), that Anna took up studies with the Open University. She completed her B.A. in 1989 with a diploma course in Business and Finance, an achievement which proved vitally useful for her later work.

"One gets asked to do things," she says with the sort of mock hopelessness which so often hides the truly determined. Initially, Anna was involved with Devon's successful N.S.P.C.C. centenary year fundraising operation, before she was invited to be Vice-President for the Newton Abbot and Moretonhampstead Centres of the Red Cross. It was work in which her idealism, practical spirit, attention to detail and capacity for hard work were to find their natural focus. She became deeply attached to the organisation and devoted an increasing amount of time to its work. "I loved its impartiality, its policy to provide skilled care for people who need it wherever and whoever they are. I felt completely at home with the Red Cross." When Anna talks about her work, there is a seriousness in her tone which suggests a total indivisibility of character and its fulfilment. Here is a woman who knows what she is about—and what she is about is helping people.

Since 1988 she has been President of the Devon Branch and Chairman of the Devon Trustee Committee. She is also a member of the National Council as well as Chairman of the newly created Regional Council. "People go around thinking I do nothing but make gracious speeches and receiving bunches of flowers," she says, "but its not like that at all. Its sheer hard work, almost frantic at times. A huge number of meetings, travelling all over Devon and beyond, usually over a thousand hours a year." Yet her family are solidly behind her present work, as was her only sister, a fully qualified nurse who died in a car accident in 1987.

After our meeting, reading the Annual Report, my eyes were opened to the scale of the services the Red Cross renders Devon: first aid cover at 1,450 events; 68 escorts for handicapped, sick and frail travellers; 3,440 home visits; 7,848 hours of Therapeutic Care and 27 call-outs related to fires, as well as the organisation of 10 shops, 19 ambulances, 30 medical equipment loan depots and 2,000 volunteers. A huge amount of this work is done by its paid staff but volunteers make an indispensable contribution. Many of these are what she describes as "unsung heroes who are great people in their own right, going that extra mile to help others. Lovely people to work with and for."

Anna is energised by her responsibilities, and positive about the future of the voluntary services. "During the path of life, when people move from one area of expertise to another there are huge opportunities to use the gaps to do voluntary work, to gain fresh experience and enjoy worthwhile and fulfilling tasks. No, caring work is not a dying, but a growing thing."

PETER SMITH

Since humankind gave up the wandering life of the hunter-gatherer, settled down to agriculture and began to live in settlements, there have been shops. Shopkeeping and shopping date back at least 5,000 years. One finds reference to 'the market street of Ur', and Enkidu's struggle with Gilgamesh took place in the 'Market of the land'. The open place or covered market, the booth or shop-lined street, had possibly found their urban form by 2000 B.C.

As the years have passed and populations have grown, shops have proportionately increased. In contemporary Devon there are at least five thousand of them; nearly 500 in Exeter; 163 in Ilfracombe and 57 in Cullompton. Outstanding amongst these are the two hardware stores that overlook Chagford's sloping Market Place: Webber's, and its neighbour James

Bowden and Son, Hardware and Moorland Centre.

The latter was founded in 1863 by a James Bowden who had come to Chagford with his son, Tom, from Meavey near Bude; he was—and remained—a shoer of horses. His daughter, Grace Bowden, developed the iron-mongery side, and in this work was later assisted by her nephew, Peter Smith. I met Peter in July 1997.

"I was fifteen when I started and I've worked here for the last forty-four years. First it was tidying up—I was paid £2 a week in those days—and then after 1953, when my father took over the shop, I helped in an increasingly substantial way. Father died in 1961 and my brother Colin and I have run the place between us ever since." In 1971, the brothers made a move which laid the foundation of their current success: they purchased Bolt's Grocers, next door. With this space they have been able to spread both sideways and backwards into Bowden's present labyrinth of tiny departments. In fact, their shop now offers everything from paraffin lamps to safety pins, extending ladders to hooks and eyes, torch batteries to wine racks, garden rakes to high-price boots and clothing. It is an Aladdin's cave, packed from floor to ceiling with an infinite variety of desirable goods.

"In the early days," says Peter Smith, "we supplied the big houses, the farmers, the retired people—it was all local trade. Nowadays it's tourism which is big business. Our peak time is August and December; about sixty per cent of our overall turnover is now with the visitor trade." Nonetheless, if this makes it sound as if running Bowden's is an easy task, Peter was enthusiastic to dis-abuse me of this notion, and in no uncertain way. "All we know is ironmongery," he told me. "It takes you over,

lock, stock and barrel. There is little life outside the shop. Colin can start at eight-thirty in the morning and go on to one o'clock at night—ordering, improving the display, sharpening scissors, forever tidying the shop. Yes, I know, its a bit old-fashioned and untidy. We sell everything you can think of, all the everyday needs—door mats, pens, cellotape, kitchen utensils, drawing pins, dog-leads, rainwear, rucksacks, light fittings, toilet paper, fishing tackle, bicycle pumps, watches, binoculars, seeds. . . you name it and we stock it. Colin and I don't know how many items we have in the shop but it could be as many as 200,000. Of course we retain a lot of the slower selling stuff as a service to our customers. We belong, you might say, to the old school. All our money is buried in stock. It's a way of life, I suppose."

Our conversation ended, I was guided to the back of the shop and its so-called 'museum', a room representing Bowden's as it is thought to have appeared in the period c.1910 to 1920. Peter had put it together and was, I think, justly proud of his labour of love. It was there that I read a newspaper article (*Sunday Express*, 1992) in which the businessman Sir John Harvey-Jones had expressed his admiration for the shop. "Whatever your interests," he is reported as saying, "you can always find something in this shop that you didn't realise you needed and yet can't imagine how you ever did without. . . such treasures as Swiss Army knives, a miniature compass, single-focus binoculars and a light for map reading." Marvelling at the availability of genuine squirrels' tails for tying fishing flies, he went on to add: "Whatever you want, they always seem to have it. I don't know how they do it. When everyone else is reducing their stock, they seem to do the opposite. It confounds all business theory and breaks every rule I know of. But I keep telling them. 'Please don't change.' Whatever they are doing has nothing to do with running a business but everything to do with keeping a fascinating shop and providing a bloody marvellous service for their customers."

PAUL WHARTON

He sails the sea; he lets down his nets for the fish in its depths and sells them from a shop in Butchers Row, a long line of them facing Barnstaple's Pannier market. He is Paul Wharton, a vigorous, hard-working, plain-spoken, independent 28-year-old who, with his brother Scott and other members of their extensive family, runs Wheatons—fishmongers and trawler owners.

The sea was their destiny: "A Devon way of life," he says. At the age of thirteen, the brothers were fishing as a hobby with nets and pots. Two years later, Paul was at the Falmouth Fishing College; six months later he was continuing his training on a 54-foot Newlyn netter fishing off the Scillies for hake and spur-dogs. Simultaneously, Scott worked on a 104-foot beamer, fishing from Brixham. At the age of eighteen, the brothers went into partnership, purchasing their first boat for £23,000, and fishing from Ilfracombe in summer and Brixham in the winter. A year later they bought a bigger boat—a 50-footer from the Orkneys—which they held for five years, fishing in the winter for lemon and Dover sole off Brixham, and for cod, ray and Dover sole from the summer seas off Ilfracombe, their home town.

Today Scott and Paul Wharton jointly own two boats: a 44-foot and a 37-foot trawler (named after Paul's daughter and Scott's son), berthed at Bideford and Ilfracombe respectively. They also provide employment for six or seven people, and own a shop in Barnstaple which provides a small retail outlet for their catch, the majority of which is bought by a Bideford wholesaler. Their modest beginnings have reaped a generous harvest.

For Paul, life at sea is demanding work but has many compensations. He loves the solidarity of the small, close-knit community on their three-day trips to sea: "You look after one another all the time; it's like a family." He loves the undisturbed peace and quiet, the time to think, the time to participate in a celebration of the sea and its seasons. "In summer," he says, "you can't beat it out there: the dolphins, Lundy, all the things around you. Fishing, you learn something new every day." Yet the work is not only absorbing, it demands a concentration of every faculty that can be utterly exhausting even for a young man in the pink of health. "Rolling around all day, I'm shattered. I'm tired out at sea and mentally drained." Fishing has always been a demanding and a precarious occupation, and always will be; hardly a year passes without young men being lost somewhere along the Devon coast. The great mother gives of her stores of fish, but never for nothing. From time to time she demands her due: a single life to herself, or at a stroke a whole ship's crew. Every eight days a man is killed at sea.

The boats, manned by crews of four, often set out before dawn. Fishing day and night, on a voyage of several days, the crew take it in turns to skipper them, to tow the nets, to haul, to gut the fish (two tons an hour), wash the catch and store it in ice. In summer the men can work a 150-hour week; in the winter, a fourteen-hour day. An average twenty-four hour period can land a hundred stone of fish, and as much as 750 stone has been caught. Yet, he says, "The old times have gone now. A boat can cost the best part of two hundred and fifty thou', so to cover that expenditure you need to work hard, very hard, very hard indeed. Fishing gets more and more difficult; decreasing stocks, competition from Spain, the regulations."

We met in their shop. Paul's wife (who worked there until her pregnancy) and another brother were serving customers, and joined in the conversation from time to time. Yet if Paul's was the commanding presence, it was apparent that the Whartons were a close-knit family whose members pulled their weight even at jobs they did

not enjoy—Paul made it clear that working in the shop is for him rather less than fulfilling, for he longs to get back to sea. He likes shooting and ferreting "to get some peace", but like his forebears (and this is the oldest industry of all), fishing is in his blood. The magic of the oceans, the oneness with nature, the intense companionship, the ecstasy of the catch, the freedom of a craft that is—at least whilst at sea—independent of the smothering restrictions of life on land, had irredeemably stolen his heart. "Fishing's always in you," he told me. "I could go on and on about fish for ever."

The people of Devon today are a mingled weave. I have selected a tiny number of them and tried to celebrate their lives, but that of Paul Wharton, as unpretentious as any, I would count amongst the most valuable. For our survival, we are dependent on the fisherman's skill, his inexhaustible dedication and his gamble with his own life. Paul, I suspect, would not see it that way—for him, fishing is a job—but without the exacting disciplines, the rigour and humility of his work, we would be the poorer. His is a life that at once enlarges and feeds our own. And of how many others can that be said?

Further Reading

GENERAL

Hoskins, W.G. *Devon*. Devon Books, 1954.

Hoskins, W.G. *Devon and its People*. A. Wheaton and Co. Ltd, 1959.

Stanes, Robin. *A History of Devon* Phillimore and Co. Ltd, 1986.

Jellicoe, Ann, & Mayne, Robin. *Devon*. Faber & Faber, 1975.

Cherry, Bridget, & Pevsner, Nikolaus. *The Buildings of England: Devon*.   Penguin Books, 1991.

Beacham, Peter, ed. *Devon Buildings: An Introduction to Local Traditions*. Devon Books, 1995.

Slader, J.M. *The Churches of Devon*. David and Charles, 1968.

Minchington, Walter. *Industrial Archæology in Devon*. Dartington Amenity Research Trust Publication Number 1, 1976.

Chapter One:

THE DEVON LANDSCAPE

THE RIVERS OF DEVON
Page, J.L.W. *The Rivers of Devon*. London, 1893.

THE COASTLINE OF DEVON
Steers, J.A. *The Coastline of England and Wales*. Cambridge University Press, 1976.

LYNTON
Mold, Ernest. *Lynton and its Coast*. Green Apple Publishing, 1992.

Lister, Raymond. *Samuel Palmer: his Life and Art*. Cambridge U.P., 1987.

CLOVELLY
Shanes, Eric. *Turner's England 1810-30*. Cassell, 1990.

DARTMOOR
Crossing, W. *Guide to Dartmoor*. Peninsula Press.

Harvey, L.A., & Gordon, D. *Dartmoor*. Collins, 1970.

Worth, R. Hansford. *Worth's Dartmoor*. Peninsula Press, 1994.

EXMOOR
MacDermot, E.T. *The History of the Forest of Exmoor*. Taunton, 1911.

Chapter Two:

ANIMAL, VEGETABLE, MINERAL

DEVONSHIRE RAIN
Keats, John. *The Letters of John Keats*. Oxford University Press, 1948.

DARTMOOR PONIES
Palmer, Joseph. *The Dartmoor Pony*. Devon Books, 1990.

GREAT TREES
Pakenham, Thomas. *Meetings with Remarkable Trees*. Weidenfeld & Nicholson, 1996.

THE DEVON LANE
Devon County Council & The Devon Hedge Group, *Devon's Hedges Conservation and Management*. Devon Books, 1997.

Rackham, O. *The History of the Countryside*. J.M. Dent, 1993.

Pollard, E., Hooper, M.D. & Moore, N.W. *Hedges* Collins, 1974.

Muir, R.N. *Hedgerows: Their History and Wildlife*. Michael Joseph, 1989.

Martin, W. Keble. *The Concise British Flora*. Ebury Press, 1965.

SOME DEVONSHIRE GARDENS
Gray, Todd. *The Garden History of Devon: An Illustrated Guide to Sources*. Univ. of Exeter Press, 1995.

Synge, Patrick. M. *The Gardens of Britain: Devon and Cornwall*. B.T. Batsford, 1977.

Pugsley, Steven. ed. *Devon Gardens: An Historical Survey* Alan Sutton Publishing Ltd, 1994.

Snell, Reginald. *From the Bare Stem: Making Dorothy Elmhirst's Garden at Dartington Hall*. Devon Books, 1989.

THE LUSTLEIGH ORCHARD
Hole, Christina. *English Folklore*. B.T. Batsford, 1940.

Chapter Three:

PLACE

EXETER
Hoskins, W.G. *Two Thousand Years in Exeter*. Phillimore, 1960.

Harvey, Hazel. *Exeter Past*. Phillimore, 1996.

Thomas, P., and Warren J. *Aspects of Exeter* 1980.

BIDEFORD
Fielder, Duncan. *A History of Bideford* Phillimore, 1985.

TORQUAY
Russell, Percy. *A History of Torquay*. Torquay Natural History Society, 1960.

Pike, John. *Torquay: The Place and the People*. Torquay Centenary Committee, 1992.

TOTNES
Russell, Percy. *The Good Town of Totnes*. Devonshire Association, 1964.

PLYMOUTH
Gill, Crispin. *A New History*. Devon Books, 1993.

Walling, R.A. *The Story of Plymouth*. 1950.

Worth, R.N. *A History of Plymouth*. 1872.

APPLEDORE
Beara, John. *Appledore: Handmaid of the Sea*.

Slade, W.J. *Out of Appledore*.

HOLY WELLS
Bord, Janet and Colin. *Sacred Waters; Holy Wells and Water Lore in Britain and Ireland*. Granada, 1985.

STONE CIRCLES ON DARTMOOR
Pettit, Paul. *Prehistoric Dartmoor*. 1974.

Butler, Jeremy. *Dartmoor Atlas of Antiquities Vol 1: The East*. Devon Books, 1991.

Burl, Aubrey. *Rings of Stone: The Prehistoric Stone Circles of Britain and Ireland*. Frances Lincoln, 1979.

A MEDIÆVAL PULPIT
Duffy, Eamon. *The Stripping of the Altars: Traditional Religion in England 1400-1580*. Yale University Press, 1992.

ST. MARY'S, ATHERINGTON
Rose, Lilian. *St. Mary's Church, Atherington* (church guide).

ST. MARY'S, HONEYCHURCH
Hoskings, W.G. *St. Mary's Church, Honeychurch* (church guide).

EXETER CATHEDRAL
Erskine, Audrey, et al. *Exeter Cathedral: A Short History and Description*. Exeter Cathedral, 1988.

Swanton, Michael ed. *Exeter Cathedral: A Celebration*. Dean and Chapter of Exeter, 1991.

DARTINGTON HALL
Emery, Anthony. *Dartington Hall*. The Clarendon Press, Oxford, 1970.

Snell, Reginald. *William Weir and Dartington Hall*. Dartington Hall Trust, 1986.

THE DARTMOOR LONGHOUSE
Beacham, Peter. ed. *Devon Buildings: An Introduction to Local Traditions*. Devon Books, 1995.

CADHAY
Anon. *Cadhay*, Devon (house guide).

LOUGHWOOD MEETING HOUSE
Anon. *Loughwood Meeting House*. The National Trust Guide.

Watts, M.R. *The Dissenters: From the Reformation to the French Revolution*. Oxford University Press, 1978.

THE ADAM ROOMS AT SALTRAM
Fletcher, Ronald. *The Parkers of Saltram 1769-1837*. B.B.C., 1970.

Stillman, Damie. *Decorative Work of Robert Adam*. London, 1973.

Dodd, Dudley. *Saltram* (house guide), The National Trust, 1996.

ALL SAINTS, BABBACOMBE
Thompson, Paul. *William Butterfield*. Routledge and Kegan Paul, 1971.

Woodford, Ian *The Parish Church of All Saints Babbacombe* (church guide).

CASTLE DROGO
Meller, Hugh. *Castle Drogo* (house guide). The National Trust, 1995.

Amery, Colin. et al. *Lutyens*. Arts Council, Hayward Gallery, London, 1981.

O'Neill, Daniel. *Sir Edwin Lutyens' Country Houses*. Lund Humphries, 1980.

THE DREAM CHURCH OF MILBER
Healey, Eileen & Boardman, John. *St. Luke's Church* (church guide).

Chapter Four:

IMAGES AND OBJECTS

A PREHISTORIC WOODEN FIGURE
Anderson, William. *Green Man: The Archetype of our Oneness with the Earth*. HarperCollins, 1990.

MEDIÆVAL IRONWORK
Lister, Raymond. *Decorative Wrought Ironwork in Great Britain*. G. Bell and Co., 1957.

BEATUS AND BOSSES
Cave, C.J.P. *Medieval Carvings in Exeter Cathedral*. Penguin Books, 1953.

Swanson, Michael. *Roof Bosses and Corbels of Exeter Cathedral*. Exeter Cathedral, 1979.

Cave, C.J.P. *Roof Bosses in Mediæval Churches*. Cambridge U. P., 1948.

Benton, Janetta. *The Medieval Menagerie*. Abbeville Press, 1992.

HARVEST JUGS
Grant, Alison. *North Devon Pottery*. University of Exeter Press, 1983.

DEVON CLOCKS
Ponsford, Clive N. *Devon Clocks and Clockmakers*. David & Charles, 1985.

HONITON LACE
Yallop, HJ. *The History of the Honiton Lace Industry*. University of Exeter Press, 1992.

Luxton, Elsie. *The Technique of Honiton Lace*. B.T. Batsford, 1979.

Pallister, Bury. *A History of Lace*. E.P. Publishing Ltd, 1976.

BLAKE AT ARLINGTON
Raine, Kathleen. *Blake and Tradition*. Princeton University Press, 1968.

THE STAVERTON PARISH MAP
Mayfield, Beatrice and Clifford, Sue. *Parish Maps*. Common Ground.

Chapter Five:

TRADITIONS

CHURCH BELLS IN DEVON
Ellacombe, H.T. *The Church Bells of Devon*. 1867.

Ingram, Tom. *Bells in England*. Frederick Muller Ltd, 1954.

Pearson, C. *Church Bells of Devon*. 1888.

DEVON CIDER
Mabey, David. *In Search of Food: Traditional Eating and Drinking in Britain*. Macdonald and James, 1978.

THE VILLAGE PUB
Bachelor, Denzil. *The English Inn*. Batsford, 1963.

Hogg, Garry. *The English Country Inn*. Batsford, 1981.

DEVONSHIRE DIALECT
Hewett, Sarah. *Peasant Speech of Devon*. Elliot Stock, 1892.

Gregory, Alfred. *Devon Verbal Provincialisms*. Gregory and Son, Palmerston Press, 1909.

Clement, Martin. *The Devon Dialect*. Clement Martin Publications, 1973.

COB AND THATCH
Clifton-Taylor, Alec. *The Pattern of English Building*. B.T. Batsford, 1962.

Egeland, Pamela. *Cob and Thatch*. Devon Books, 1988.

THE CIRCLING YEAR
Coxhead, J.R.W. *Old Devon Customs*. The Raleigh Press, Exmouth, 1957.

Whistler, Laurence. *The English Festivals*. William Heinemann, 1947.

Whitlock, Ralph. *The Folklore of Devon*. B.T. Batsford Ltd, 1977.

CLOTTED CREAM
Hartley, Dorothy. *Food in England*. Macdonald, 1954.

Mabey, David. *In Search of Food: Traditional Eating and Drinking in Britain*. Macdonald and James, 1978.

SONG AND DANCE

Baring-Gould, S., and Fleetwood-Sheppard, Rev H., *Songs and Ballads of the West*. Methuen and Co, 1892; in four parts 1891-5.

Reeves, James, *The Everlasting Circle: English Traditional Verse*. Heinemann, 1960.

Chapter Six:

OCCUPATIONS

Minchington, Walter. *Devon at Work*. David and Charles, 1974

FARMING

Hicks, Norman. *Farming in the West*. Donald Rendel Ltd, 1968.

Hoskins W.G. *History from the Farm*. Faber and Faber, 1970.

Stratton, J. M. *Agricultural Records A.D. 220-1977*. John Baker, 1969.

Martin. E.W. *The Secret People: English Village Life after 1750*. Phoenix House Ltd, 1954.

MINING AND EXTRACTION

Barton, D.B. *History of Copper Mining in Cornwall and Devon*. D. Bradford Barton, Truro, 1961.

Booker, Frank. *The Industrial Archaeology of the Tamar Valley*, 1971.

THE CLOTH INDUSTRY

Hoskins, W.G. *Industry, Trade and People in Exeter, 1688-1800*. Manchester University Press, 1935.

Ponting, K.G. *The Woollen Industry of the South West England*. Adams and Dart, 1971.

Mann, J de L. *The Cloth Industry in the West of England 1640-1880*. Clarendon Press, Oxford 1971.

FISHING

Dickinson M.G. *A Living from the Sea: Devon's Fishing Industry and its Fishermen*. Devon Books, 1987.

Oppenheim, M. *The Maritime History of Devon*. 1968.

Duffy, Michael et al *The New Maritime History of Devon Vol I: From Early Times to the Late Eighteenth Century*. Conway Maritime Press in association with the University of Exeter Press, 1992.

Duffy, Michael and others. *The New Maritime History of Devon Vol II: From the Eighteenth Century to the Present Day*. Conway Maritime Press etc, 1994.

THE BUILDING INDUSTRY

Gimpel, Jean. *The Cathedral Builders*. The Cresset Library, 1988.

Knoop, D. and Jones, G.P. *The Mediæval Mason*. Manchester University Press, 1967.

THE GREAT WESTERN RAILWAY

St. John Thomas, David. *Regional History of the Railways of Great Britain: Vol I, The West Country*. David and Charles, 1988.

Rolt, L.T.C. *Isambard Kingdom Brunel*. Book Club Associates, 1972.

Booker, Frank. *The History of the G.W.R.*, 1977.

Chapter Seven:

DEVONSHIRE CHARACTERS

ARSCOTT OF TETCOTT

Hawker, R.S. *Footprints of Former Men in Far Cornwall*. Bodley Head, 1908.

Baring-Gould, Sabine. *Devonshire Characters and Strange Events* (First Series).

ROBERT HERRICK

Moorman, F.W. *Robert Herrick: A Biographical and Critical Study*. John Lane, The Bodley Head.

Martin, L.C. *Poetical Works of Robert Herrick*. 1956.

SABINE BARING-GOULD

Dickinson, Bickford H.C. *Sabine Baring-Gould*. David and Charles, 1970.

HENRY WILLIAMSON

Williamson, Henry. *Tarka the Otter*. Webb and Bower, 1985.

Williamson, Henry. *Life in a Devon Village*. Faber, 1945.

Williamson, Henry. *Tales of a Devon Village*. Faber, 1945.

Williamson, Henry. *Goodbye West Country*, Putnam. 1937.

Farson, Daniel. *Henry Williamson— a Portrait*. Robinson Publishing, 1986.

Bruce, Sylvia et al. *Henry Williamson—The Man, The Writings: A Symposium*. Tabb House, 1980.

Williamson, Anne. *Henry Williamson*. Alan Sutton Publishing, 1995.

SHEILA CASSIDY

Cassidy, Sheila. *Audacity to Believe*. Darton, Longman and Todd., 1992.

Cassidy, Sheila. *The Loneliest Journey*. Darton, Longman and Todd, 1991.

Cassidy, Sheila *Good Friday People*. Darton, Longman and Todd.

Cassidy, Sheila *From the Dark Valley*. Darton, Longman and Todd

JAMES LOVELOCK

Lovelock, James. *Gaia: a new look at life on Earth*. Oxford University Press, 1979.

Lovelock, James. *The Ages of Gaia*. W.W. Norton, 1988.

Lovelock, James. *Gaia: the practical science of planetary medicine*. Gaia Books, 1991.

Wolpert, Lewis. *Passionate Minds*. Oxford University Press, 1997.

Allaby, Michael. *Guide to Gaia*. Optima, 1989.

JOHN MOAT

Moat, John. *The Missing Moon*. Green Books, 1986.

Moat, John. *Firewater & the Miraculous Mandarin*. Enitharmon Press, 1990.

Moat, John. *Practice*. Libanus Press, 1994.

Moat, John. *The Valley*. Libanus Press, 1998.

Index

Abbotskerswell 82
Abbott, John White 105
Aclands of Hawkridge Barton
  125
Adam, Robert 80–1
Aelfwold, Bishop of Crediton 32
Alfington 82
All Saints, Babbacombe 82, 83
All Saints, North Molton **88**
Allan, John 92
Appledore 56–7, **136**
  Bude Street **56**, 56
  Irsha Street 56
  Maritime Museum 57, 99
  Market Street 56
  shipbuilding 56
apples 40, 41, 115, 143
  see also cider
Arlington Court 104, 105
Arscott, John 148–9
Arscotts of Tetcott 148–9
arsenic mining 25, 132, 133
Arvon Foundation 168
Ash, Maurice 143
Ashburton 32–3, 140
  Christmas Mumming Plays 123
  cloth industry 135
  St. Gudula's Well 61
  tin 25
Ashen faggot 123
Ashprington
  Sharpham House 80
  Sharpham Vineyard **142**, 143
Ashton 68
Ashwell **14**
Atherington, St. Mary's 66–7
Auden, W.H. 145
Austen, Jane 15, 30
Axe river 17
Axmouth 137

Babbacombe
  All Saints **82**, 82, **83**, 83
  St. John's 82
Badgworthy Water 26
Bampton 138
  Horse Fair 127
Baptist chapels 79
Baring-Gould, Sabine 113, 127, 146,
  148, 149–50
Barker, Reg 58–9
Barle river 26
Barnstaple 15, 141
  castle 138
  C.H. Brannam Ltd 154
  North Devon Athenaeum 99
  pottery 98, 99
Bassett, Sir Ralph and Lady Elinor
  66
Beacham, Peter 75
Beaford church **139**
Beaumaris castle, Wales 138
Beer 19
  fishing 137
  lace-making 102, 103
Beer Head 19
Bellchambers, J.K. 101
bells 110–11
  call-change ringing 110
Bennett, Bill 52–3
Bere Alston 82
Berry Pomeroy 138
Berrynarbor, The Olde Globe 117
bestiaries 97
Bicton 34
Bideford 15, **48**, 49, 141
  Bridgeland Street 49
  Burton Art Gallery 99
  Elizabeth period 49
  fishing 137
  Long Bridge **49**

pottery 98, 99
Binyon, Laurence 89
birds 58
Black John **148**, 149
Blackawton Brewery, South Hams
  143
Blackmore, R.D. 26, 105
blacksmiths, medieval period 94–5
Blake, William 105
  The Sea of Time and Space **104**,
  105
Blanchdown 132
Blundell, Peter 135
Bolt Head 19
Booker, Frank 133
Bourne, Ivor 152–4
Bovey river 17
Bovey Tracey, Christmas
  Mumming Plays 123
Bowden's farm **74**
Bowen, Clive 154–5
Braddons 50
Bramich, Mick 127
Branscombe, lace-making 102
Braunton Burrows 18
Bray river 17
Bridford 65
Brixham 19
  fishing 137
  harbour **128**
Broad Clyst 38
  Christmas Mumming Plays 123
Broadhembury
  thatched cottages **121**
  The Drewe Arms 117
Bronze Age 32, 37
bronze figures, Roman 92, **93**
Brunel, Isambard Kingdom 140,
  141
Buckland in the Moor 65

Buck's Mills 18
Budleigh Salterton 19, 137
building industry 138–9
Burl, Aubrey 63
Burton Art Gallery, Bideford 99
Bute, Marchioness of 21
Butter Hill 18
Butterfield, William 80, 82

Cadhay **76**, 77
  Court of Sovereigns **77**, 77
cairns 62
calendar events *see* festivals and
  feast days
Calvert, Edward 57
The Cyder Feast 57, **114**
Caractacus stone 26
Carey river 17
Carpenter Oak and Woodland Co.
  159–60
Carson, Rachel 164
Cary, George 22
Cassidy, Sheila 155–8, 172
Castle Drogo 80, **84**, 84–5
Castlehill 34
castles 138
  Exeter 46, 138
  Norman 46, 52
celebrations *see* festivals and feast
  days
Celts 61, 90–1
  missionaries 61
  saints 61
Centre for Alternative Technology
  158
Centwine, Saxon King 32
Chagford 25, 180–2
  tin 25
Chains, The 26
chapels, Nonconformist 79

see also churches
Chichester family 66
china clay pits 25, 42–3, 133
Chippendale, Thomas 80
Chittlehampton 65
  St. Urith procession 123
Chope, Thomas 98
Christian missionaries 61
Christmas Mumming Plays 123
Chronicle of Ancient Sunlight, A
151, 152
Chulmleigh 111, 140
  Old Fair 123
Church House, Rattery 117
churches 61, 65–9, 80, 82–3, 86–7
  bells 110–11
  bosses 96–7
  building 138–9
  carpentry 66
  decorating 113
  Easter 113
  Elizabethan period 79
  Exeter 47
  fonts 95
  Green Man carvings 91, 96
  Harvest Festival **108**, 113
  Loughwood Meeting House **78**,
    79
  mediæval period **64**, 65, 66, 68,
    95, 96, 138
  1930s 86–7
  Nonconformist chapels 79
  Norman period 65, 68, 71, 95
  pulpits **64**, 65, 95
  Victorian period 82–3
  see also Exeter Cathedral
cider 114–15
  orchards 40, 41, 115
Cistercian abbeys
  Tavistock 124
  Vale Royal, Cheshire 138
cists 62
Citadel, Plymouth 55

Clapworthy Mill 115
Clement, William 101
climate 15, 18, 25, 30, 34, 50, 51
clocks **100**, 100–1, **101**
cloth industry 52, 134–5
clotted cream 124–5
Clovelly 21, **22**, 22–3, 137
Clyst river 17
coaching inns 117
coastal forts 26
  see also forts
coastline 18–19, 26
cob and thatch cottages 120–1
Cockington 50
Coleford, thatched cottages **121**
Coleridge, Samuel Taylor 21, 105,
  146
Coleton Fishacre 38–9
  Rill Garden **38**
Collins, Cecil 105, 142
Colyford 124
Colyton 14, 102
Combe Martin
  fishing 137
  The Hunting of the Earl of
    Rone 123
Conan Doyle, Sir Arthur 166
Congregationalist chapels 79
copper mining 25, 42, 132–3
Cornworthy **59**
  Parish Book 58–9
Cott, The, Dartington 117
cottages 75, 120–1
Coutts, Thomas 21
Cowley, John 42
crab fishing 137
Crediton 140, 141
cromlechs 62
Cromwell, Oliver 130
Crossing, William 25
Cullompton, St. Andrew's **134**,
  135
Culmstock, cloth industry 135

Dalch river 17
Dalwood, Loughwood Meeting
  House **78**, 79
dancing 126, 127
Dart
  river **17**, 17, 52, 65, 143
  valley 142
Dart, Robert 171
Dartington
  Christmas Mumming Plays 123
  The Cott Inn 117
Dartington Hall **72**, 73
  courtyard **73**
  gardens 38, 39, 73
  Tiltyard 39
Dartmoor 15, 17, **24**, 25
  early settlement 25
  grazing rights 33
  Iron Age hillforts 25
  longhouses **74**, 75
  mining 25
  natural history 25
  ponies 32–3
  stone circles 62–3
  Wistman's Wood 34, **35**
Dartmouth 65
  Butterwalk 95
  The Carved Angel 170–1
  St. Clement's 95
  St. Petrox 95
  St. Saviour's 65, **94**, 95, **95**
Dawlish 19, 30
  Luscombe Castle 80
Dawlish Warren 141
Dean Prior 146, 147
deep-sea fishing 137
Defoe, Daniel 49, 52
Densham Farm **131**
Devil's Boulder, Shebbear 123
Devon Christian Ecology Group
  172
Devon Great Consols 132–3
Devonport, Ker Street 55

Devonshire Great Consolidated
  Copper Mining Company 132
dialect 119
Dickens, John 42
Dira Farm 174–6
Dissenters 79
dissolution of the monasteries 77
Dittisham 65
  St. George's **64**, 65
dockyards 55
Doddiscombsleigh, The Nobody
  Inn 117
dolmens 62
Dolton 65
  St. Edmund's **111**
Domesday Book 34, 68
Dornafield Farmyard **130**
Dowland, St. Peter's **108**
Down, Roger 66
Down St. Mary 111
D'Oyly Carte, Rupert and Lady
  Dorothy 38
Drake's island 55
Drewe, Julius 84
Drewe Arms, Broadhembury 117
Drewsteignton 171, 173
Drizzlecombe, stone rows **44**]
Duke of York, Iddesleigh **116**, 117

East Dean river 25
East Webburn river **16**
East Woolfardisworthy 82
East-the-Water 49
Eastlake, Charles 105
Edwardian period
  Plymouth 55
  Torquay 51
Elephant's Nest, Horndon **117**
Elizabethan period
  Appledore 56
  Bideford 49
  churches 79
Elmhirst, Dorothy 38

English China Clays 42
Equation Clock, Powderham **101**, 101
Erme river 17
Exe Plain 26
Exe river 17, 25, 26
Exeter 35, 46–7
  castle 138
  Christmas Mumming Plays 123
  churches 47
  cloth industry 134, 135
  Georgian architecture 47
  Guildhall 47
  mediæval period 47
  Norman period 46, 47
  railways 140
  Roman period 92
  Royal Albert Memorial Museum 99
Exeter Cathedral **70**, **71**, 71, 138
  bosses 96–7
  Green Man carvings 91, 96
  mediæval period 71
  Norman period **70**, 71
  Psalter **97**, 97
Exmoor 15, 26–7, **27**
  Forest 26
  streams 26
Exmouth
  fishing 137
  lace-making 103

farming 130–1, 134, 152–4, 161, 174–6
festivals and feast days 40–1, 123, 126
  fire festivals **122**, 123
  Harvest Festival **108**, 113
  May Day celebrations 40–1, 126
Finchingfield, Essex 103
fire festivals **122**, 123
  see also festivals and feast days
fishing 50, 56, 136–7, 182–3

Fitz's Well **60**
Fleet river 50
folk-dancing 126, **127**, 127
folk-songs 126–7, 150
food production 143
  cider-making 114–15
  clotted cream 124–5
  wine-making 143
Foreland Point 18
Fortescue, Katherine and Lionel 38
forts, Roman 25, 26, 92
Fremington clay 98

Gaia 163
Garden House, The 38, 39
gardens 38–9, 73
geology 15
Georgeham
  Skirr Cottage **151**
  Spreacombe Iron Works **132**
Georgian architecture
  Appledore 56
  Exeter 47
Gidleigh 138
Gill, Eric 155
Girtin, Thomas 56–7
  Appledore, North Devon **57**
Godwin, William 21
gold mining 132
Golding, William 164
Goodchild, H.E. 160
Gothic age 95
granite quarrying 42
Great Western Railway 140–1
Green Man carvings 91
  Exeter Cathedral 91, 96
Greenway, John 135
Grenville, Sir Richard 49
Grey Wethers **62**, 62
gunpowder-making 42

Haggard, H. Rider 13
Hamlyn, Christine 23

Hancock, Norman 115
Hangingstone Hill 62, **63**
Harberton 65
Hard, Robert 127
Harrison, Reverend William 22
Hartland 68
Hartland Point 18–19
Hartley, Ben 36
Harvest Festival **108**, 113
harvest jugs **98**, 98–9, **99**
Harvest Thanksgiving 113
Harvey, John 95
Harvey-Jones, Sir John 181–2
Hatherleigh Fire Festival 123
Hawker, Robert Stephen 113, 148, 149
Hawkridge Barton, Acland family 125
Hawkridge Farm, Umberleigh 124–5
Haydon, Benjamin Robert 105
Haydon, John 77
Hayward, John 82
Heathcoat, John 102
hedgerows 37, 68
Hegel, G.W.F. 129
Heineken, N.S. 92
Hemyock 138
Hennock 65
Hercules Promontory 19
Herrick, Robert 105, 146–7
herring fishing 137
High Bickington 91
  Kingford Hall **127**
High Cross House 87
High Willhays 25
hill forts 25
  see also forts
Hilliard, Nicholas 105
Hittisleigh, St. Andrew's **172**
Holland, John 73
Holmes, Richard 146
Holne 65

Holsworthy 14, 141
holy wells 61, 113
Honeychurch, St. Mary's 68, **69**
Honiton
  cloth industry 135
  lace 102–3
Hooker, John 114
  map of Exeter 46, 47
Hooker, Richard 105
Hopkins, Gerard Manley 29, 83
Horndon, The Elephant's Nest **117**
Hosking, Valerie and John 124–5
Hoskins, W.G. 17, 37, 47, 52, 68, 114, 131, 137, 138, 152
Hound of the Baskervilles 166
Hudson, Thomas 105
Hudson, W.H. 107
Hughes, Ted 146, 152
Huish, St. James the Less **31**
Huna 68
Hunting of the Earl of Rone, Combe Martin 123
hut-circles 62
Hutchinson, Peter Orlando 92
Hyll, John 66

Iddesleigh, The Duke of York **116**, 117
Ilfracombe 18, 137
Iron Age hillforts 25
iron mining 25, 132
ironwork, medieval period 94–5

James, Roderick and Gillie 158–60
Jones, David 9

Keats, John 30
Kenn river 17
Kenton 65
Killerton House 38, 126
Kilvert, Francis 45
Kingford Hall, High Bickington **127**

King's Nympton 68, 91
    St. James' **110**
Kingsland, Reg and Hazel 160–2
Kingsley, Charles 22, 105
Kingsteignton 42, 90
Kingswear 137
Knight, John 27
Knighthayes Court 34, 38

lace 102–3
Ladywell 61
Lammas festival 113
Landkey, cloth industry 135
Lane, John 135
lanes 36–7
language 119
Lank Combe 26
Lawrence, D.H. 8
Le Corbusier 85
lead mining 25, 42, 132
Lee Moor 25
Lee Moor Clay Works 42–3, **43**
Lescaze, William 87
Lew river 17
Lew Trenchard 149, 150
    St. Peter's **150**
Lobb, Mark 171
longhouses, Dartmoor **74**, 75
Lorna Doone 26
Loudon, J.C. 35
Loughwood Meeting House **78**, 79
Lovelock, James and Sandy 162–4
Lucan 90–1
Lucombe oaks **34**, 34–5
Lundy 19
Luscombe Castle, Dawlish 80
Lustleigh 40–1
    May Day 40–1
    orchard 40, **41**, 41
Lutyens, Sir Edwin 80, 84–5
Lydford 25, 138
Lyn Cleave 21
Lynmouth Bay 18, 21

Lynn, Manuela and Mike 171
Lynton 20–1, 168, 169
    Ladywell 61

Manning, Aaron 117
Maritime Museum, Appledore 57, 99
Marshall, James 165–6
Martin, Arthur 87
Martin, Rev J. Keble 87
Martin, W. Keble 37
Marzials, Theo 14
Massingham, H.J. 160
May Day celebrations 40–1, 126
    see also festivals and feast days
Maypoles 40, 41
Meavy Oak 34
Medici, Cosimo de 102
mediæval period
    bosses **96**, 96–7
    building 138
    churches **64**, 65, 66, 68, **95**, 96, 138
    Dartington Hall 73
    Dartmoor 25
    Exeter 47
    Exeter Cathedral 71
    farming 130
    hedges 37
    ironwork 94–5
    lanes 37
    longhouses **74**, 75
    pottery 155
megalithic tombs 62
menhirs 62
Mere river 17
Methodist chapels 79
    Providence Chapel **79**
Middlecott **2**
Milber, St. Luke's **86**, 87
Miller, W., *Clovelly Bay* **23**
mining
    arsenic 25, 132, 133

china clay pits 25, 42–3, 133
copper 25, 42, 132–3
Dartmoor 25
gold 132
iron 25, 132
lead 25, 42, 132
silver 42, 132
Tavistock 133
tin 25, 42, 132
wolfram 132
zinc 42
Misselbrook, Susan 107
missionaries
    Celtic 61
    Christian 61
Moat, John 166–8
Modbury 111
Mold, Ernest 168–9
Molland 68
Molyneux, Joyce 170–1
monasteries
    Cistercian abbeys 124, 138
    dissolution of 77
Moretonhampstead 25
Morris, William 133
Morwellham **133**, 133
Morwenstow 113
mosses 59
Mount Edgcumbe 55
Mumming Plays 123

Napier, Charles 171–3
Nash, John 80
natural history 58–9
    birds 58
    Dartmoor 25
    hedgerows 37
    mosses 59
    oak trees 34–5, 39, 58
    trees 34–5, 39, 58, 59
    wild flowers 19, 37, 59
    wildlife 37, 58, 59
naval dockyards 55

Newton, Sir Isaac 41
Newton Abbot 141
Nobody Inn, Doddiscombsleigh 117
Nonconformist chapels 79
Norman period
    castles 46, 52
    churches 65, 68, 71, 95
    Exeter **46**, 47
    Exeter Cathedral **70**, 71
    forest law 26–7
North Bovey 91
    Sanders, Lettaford 75
North Devon Athenaeum, Barnstaple 99
North Devon Maritime Museum 99
North Molton
    All Saints **88**
    church bells 111
North Tawton **28**, 92, 141
Northcote, James 105
Nuthall, Vanessa and Ady 174–6
Nutwell 138

oak trees 34–5, 39, 58
Okehampton 17, 92, 138, 141
    Fitz's Well **60**, 61
Okement river 17
Olde Globe, Berrynarbor 117
orchards 40, 41, 115, 143
Otterton 137
Ottery St. Mary 82, 146
    Cadhay 76–7
    lace-making 102
Outer Froward Point 19

Paignton 19
painters 21, 23, 80, 105
Palmer, Samuel, *From the Castle Hotel Lynton* **20**, 21
Park Hill 50
Parker, John (Lord Borington) 80

Parracombe 68
   holy well of St. Thomas 61
Parson, James 127
Peagham Barton **118**
Pearson, John Loughborough 67
Perkins brothers 160
Peters Marland 98
Pevsner, Nikolaus 52, 65, 73, 85
Phear Park **34**, 35
Pike, James 160
Plym river 42
Plymouth 19, 42, **54**, 55
   Barbican 55
   Citadel 55
   fishing 137
   housing 55
   naval dockyards 55
   railways 141
   Royal Citadel 55
   Royal William Victualling Yard
      55, 139
   Sound 19
   war damage 55
Plymouth Hoe 55
Plympton 138
poets 21, 30, 146–7
ponies 32–3
Ponsford, Clive N. 100
population 130, 131
pottery 154–5
   harvest jugs **98**, 98–9, **99**
Powderham 138
   Equation Clock **101**, 101
prehistoric era 90–1
   cairns 62
   cists 62
   Dartmoor 25
   Exmoor 26
   hedgerow system 37
   hut-circles 62
   megalithic tombs 62
   menhirs 62
   monuments 26, 37

standing stones 62
stone circles 26, 62–3
stone rows **44**, 62
wooden sculptures 90–1, **91**
Princetown 141
Prout, Samuel 105
Providence Methodist Chapel **79**
Ptolemy 19
pubs 116–17
Pudcombe Cove 38
pulpits **64**, 65, 95

Rafferty, Sean and Peggy 117
railways 140–1
rain 30–1
Raine, Kathleen 105
Randall-Page, Peter 176–8
Rattery, The Church House 117
red clay 98, 154
Reddaway, Jose 68
Reed Hall 35
Reeves, James 127
Rennie, John 55
Reynolds, John Hamilton 30
Reynolds, Sir Joshua 80, 105
Richmond Dry Dock 56
Rill Garden **38**
ritual 123
   see also festivals and feast days
Riverford Farm, South Hams 143
rivers 16–17, 25
Robertson, Anna 178–80
Rockall, Samuel 160
Roman period 32, 92–3
   bronze figure 92, **93**
   Christianity 61
   Exeter 92
   Exmoor 26
   forts 25, 26, 92
   tabernae vinariae 117
Rosemoor 38
round barrows 26
Rowe, Reverend Samuel 62

Royal Albert Bridge, Saltash 141
Royal Albert Memorial Museum,
   Exeter 99
Royal Horticultural garden, Royal
William Victualling Yard,
   Plymouth 55, 139

St. Andrew's, Cullompton **134**, 135
St. Andrew's, Hittisleigh **172**
St. Clement's, Dartmouth 95
St. Edmund's, Dolton **111**
St. George's, Dittisham **64**, 65
St. Gudula's Well, Ashburton 61
St. James', King's Nympton **110**
St. James the Less, Huish **31**
St. John's, Babbacombe 82
St. Luke's, Milber **86**, 87
St. Marychurch 50
St. Mary's, Atherington 66–7
St. Mary's, Honeychurch 68, **69**
St. Morwenna, holy well 113
St. Nectan 61
   holy wells **61**, 61
St. Peter's, Dowland **108**
St. Peter's, Lew Trenchard **150**
St. Peter's, Tiverton **135**
St. Petrox, Dartmouth 95
St. Saviour's, Dartmouth 65, **94**, 95,
   95
St. Urith procession 123
saints 61
Salcombe 137
Salcombe Estuary 19
Saltash, Royal Albert Bridge 141
Saltram House 139
   the Adam rooms 80–1, **81**
Sampford Courtenay 68, 91
Sanders, Lettaford, North Bovey 75
Saxons 32
Scorhill 62, **63**, 63
Scott, Reverend Prebendary John
   110–11
sculpture 176–8

prehistoric 90–1, **91**
Seaton 19, 102, 137
Sessions, Barry 40
severed head, cult of 61
Sharkham Point 19
Sharman, Mark 143
Sharp, Cecil 126
Sharpham House 80
Sharpham Vineyard, Ashprington
   142, 143
Shaugh Moor 32
Shebbear 154
   turning the Devil's Boulder 123
Shelley, Percy Bysshe 21, 26
shipbuilding 56
   Appledore 56
   naval dockyards 55
   Plymouth 56
shops 51, 180–2
Sidbury 102
Sidmouth 19, 30
   Christmas Mumming Plays 123
   fishing 137
   lace-making 102
silver mining 42, 132
Silverton, Christmas Mumming
   Plays 123
singing 126–7
Skirr Cottage, Georgeham **151**
Slapton Ley 19
Slapton sands 19
Smeaton lighthouse 55
Smith, Peter 180–2
Snell, Anthony 66
Society of Friends' meeting houses
   79
South Brent 34
South Cliff, Ladywell 61
South Devon Railway 140–1
South Hams 14, **142**, 143
South Molton 140
   cloth industry 135
South Tawton 91, 111, 160

Southey, Robert 21
speech 119
Spicelands 79
Spreacombe Iron Works,
	Georgeham **132**
Spreyton 91
standing stones 62
	see also stone circles; stone rows
Start, the 19
Staverton parish map **106**, 107
step dancing 127
Stewart, Jamie 117
Sticklepath 34
Stoke, holy well of St. Nectan 61
Stoke Canon 65
Stoke Gabriel, Christmas
	Mumming Plays 123
stone circles 26
	Dartmoor 62–3
	Grey Wethers **62**, 62
	Scorhill 62, **63**, 63
stone rows 62
	Drizzlecombe **44**
Street, G.E. 80, 82
Stuart period, farming 130
Stubbes, Philip 40
Stumbels, William 101
Sturt, George 100
Swimbridge 65

Tamar
	as boundary 17
	river 17, 25
	valley 132
Tapeley Park 38
Tarka the Otter 151–2
Tavistock
	church bells 111
	Cistercian abbey 124
	clotted cream making 124
	copper mining 133
	Goosey Fair 127
	railways 141

tin 25
Taw
	estuary 18, 98
	river 17
Taylor, Sir Robert 80
Teign river 17
Teignmouth 19, 30, 141
	herring fishing 137
Tetcott 148–9
thatched cottages **120**, 120–1, **121**
thatching 165–6
tin mining 25, 42, 132
Tiverton 14
	castle 138
	Christmas Mumming Plays 123
	church bells 111
	cloth industry 135
	lace-making 102
	St. Peter's **135**
Topsham 137
Tor Bay 50, 51
Torbay **19**
Torbryan 68
Tor Mohun 50
Torquay 19, 50–1
	Hesketh Crescent 50
Torr, Cecil 119
Torridge
	estuary 18, 98
	river 17, 25, 49
Torrington 141
	fire festival **122**
	May Fair 123
Totnes 52–3, **53**
	castle 138
	church bells 111
	cloth industry 135
	Fore Street 52
	Guildhall 52
	High Street 52
tourism 19, 21, 22, 25, 50–1
Towne, Francis 105
tree worship 90

trees 34–5, 39, 58, 59
Tudor period
	Cadhay 76–7
	Totnes Guildhall 52
Turkey oaks 34, 39
Turner, J.M.W. 23
Twitchen on Exmoor 82

Ugborough 91
Umberleigh, Hawkridge Farm
	124–5
Unitarian chapels 79
Upper Badgworthy valley 26
urbanisation 130–1

Valley of the Rocks 21
Victorian period
	Appledore 56
	churches 82–3
	Torquay 51

Waldon 50
	river 17
Walker, John Rawson, *A View of*
	Torquay **51**
watchmakers 100–1
Weil, Simone 9
Weir, William 73
Welcombe 113
	holy well of St. Nectan 61
wells *see* holy wells
West Lyn river 26
West Ogwell 68
West Webburn river **16**
Westcote, Thomas 22, 102
Westminster Abbey 138
Westward Ho 18
Wharton, Paul 182–3
Wheal Emma 133
Whistler, Laurence 109
white ball clay 98
Whitestone Farm, South Hams
	143

wild flowers 19, 37, 59
wildlife 37, 58, 59
William of Montacute 96
Williamson, Henry 151–2
wine-making 143
Winkleigh **121**
Winsford Hill, Somerset 26
Wistman's Wood 34, **35**
wolfram mining 132
wooden sculptures, prehistoric
	90–1, **91**
Woody Bay 18
Woolacombe 18
woollen cloth-making 134–5
Wordsworth, William 21
Worth, R. Hansford 25
writers 21, 22, 105, 151–2, 166–8

Yealm river 17
Yealmpton 82
Yelverton 141
Yeo, James 56
Yes Tor 25
Youens, William 160
Young, Arthur 43

zinc mining 42
Zitherixon, Kingsteignton 90